The Modern Chair

The Modern Chair
Classics in production

Clement Meadmore

VNR **VAN NOSTRAND REINHOLD COMPANY**
NEW YORK CINCINNATI TORONTO LONDON MELBOURNE

Library of Congress Catalog Card Number 74-17853
ISBN 0-442-25303-6

Printed in the United States of America.

Paperback edition published in 1979 by
Van Nostrand Reinhold Company
A division of Litton Educational Publishing, Inc.
135 West 50th Street, New York, NY 10020, U.S.A.

Van Nostrand Reinhold Limited
1410 Brichmount Road
Scarborough, Ontario M1P 2E7, Canada

Van Nostrand Reinhold Australia Pty. Ltd.
17 Queen Street
Mitcham, Victoria 3132, Australia

Van Nostrand Reinhold Company Limited
Molly Millars Lane
Wokingham, Berkshire, England

16 15 14 13 12 11 10 9 8 7 6 5 4 3

Contents

Introduction

The aim of this book is to show that certain chairs, through a combination of practical qualities and elegance, have transcended the confines of time and fashion. The sense in which each chair belongs to its period is not of primary interest to me here, and so I shall not take into account the art historian's considerations of fashion. I shall show that though several of the chairs have marked connections with twentieth century movements in fine and applied art — Constructivism and Art Nouveau, for example — none of them, however radical its design is merely an exercise in a style imposed by contemporary taste. Each chair, then, has been selected for qualities that we can assess from our standpoint today; qualities which have less to do with style and period than with a solution of a defined problem. I have tried to explain each problem, and the consequent significance of the designer's solution (bearing in mind the limitations imposed by techniques and materials available at the time) and to discuss its contemporary relevance.

The continued production of each chair will be justified on design alone. I do not feel that indiscriminate reproduction in any past style is justified, because I do not accept nostalgia as a legitimate reason for prolonging and extending the availability of any object through mass-production. When we decide to continue producing what is supposed to be a classic design, we should make sure that it really serves our needs today as it was first designed, and not in some up-dated, modified or 'improved' form. If up-dating is needed, we are at the point of recognizing a new possibility and we would do better to create a new design. Some of the chairs here *have* undergone minor modifications, but the basic concept of the designer has not been altered, and in no way are the modifications parallel to the kind of production changes made upon antique originals by the mass-production 'hand-carved' manufacturers.

The chairs selected are not all fully machine made, nor are they all made in quantity, but with only one exception they are all available in some form of current production. Certain designs, such as those of Breuer and Le Corbusier, have had a lapse between initial and revived production, and this fact may seem to disqualify them from the requirement of timelessness, but I believe that they will now be in production for many years. The lapse in the popularity of furniture designed by Breuer and others in the pre-war period was caused by an oversight on the part of those who decide what will sell (they must have been dismayed by the avant-garde nature of Bauhaus designs) and by the total disruption of the new trends that were then emerging in Europe, by the outbreak of the Second World War.

I have tried to avoid too much vague talk of aesthetics, but it is difficult not to retire into one's own aesthetic vocabulary when looking at these chairs. I am reminded of Van Doesberg's description of Rietveld's chairs: 'the abstract-real sculpture of our future interior'. Some of the finer adjustments of proportion, left unresolved by the mere solving of functional problems, have often been made with a visual sensitivity which undoubtedly contributes to make a chair a delightful object, and to enhance its purely formal significance. It can even be said in some cases that visual considerations have led to fresh ideas, and have demanded the use of new materials and methods — invention having perhaps been the mother of necessity.

Certain of these chairs are kept on the market by people who buy them for the name of their famous creator, or for the implication of design integrity they are thought to confer. I hope that perhaps a greater understanding of the chairs real qualities may make for a less precious attitude to good design, and for a less unquestioning acceptance of the status-symbol chair as a kind of stylistic name-dropping. More important, I hope that a real appreciation of these chairs will lead to a demand for new designs that are the result of genuine effort at a high creative level to solve the problems of chair design.

The scale drawings in this book are all one-eighth of full size, so that dimensions can be ascertained by direct measurement, and comparisons can be made at a constant scale.

Part 1 Classics

The classic chairs, for the purpose of this book, are those designed between the beginnings of the modern movement and the Second World War and which survive in production to the present day. Within this area I have selected those which I consider to be innovative and influential in a positive way. In most cases they were the first examples of what has now become a familiar type in the idiom of modern furniture.

I have included more than one example of cantilever chairs, partly because it is not absolutely clear which was the first of its kind, and because they each show significant differences, in rationale and aesthetic. Mies van der Rohe, for instance, thought of the cantilever primarily as a graceful spring, whereas Marcel Breuer saw it as a simplification of the old idea of four legs (p. 47). Alvar Aalto, on the other hand, was involved with the exploitation of the potential of newly available laminated wood, with its great strength in curved configurations (p. 85).

The other classics included here nearly all show interesting affinities with contemporary fine art movements, showing the extent to which their designers were involved with painters, sculptors and industrial and graphic artists of their own time. Rietveld's chairs (pp. 36, 93, 154) are closely connected with De Stijl; Breuer's express the Bauhaus aesthetic (p. 53). Tatlin's chair is related to his constructivist sculpture, and to his experiments with the basic laws of structure (p. 49). Riemerschmid was a member of the Art Nouveau movement, and its urbane atmosphere permeates the detailing of his chair (p. 25).

Bentwood armchair

Michael Thonet

Austria, 1870

In 1840 Michael Thonet invented a process for bending wood which revolutionized the mass production of furniture. He soon established a range of bentwood chairs and other furniture running into hundreds of variations, of which the example shown here is perhaps the most elegant. His patented process consisted of clamping a thin flexible strip of steel along one side of a piece of steamed wood. This side, after bending, became the outside of the curve. Without steel, compression of the inner edge and tension on the outer would result in the outside cracking on the curve. This simple process enabled Thonet to use extremely tight structural curves, just as strong or even stronger than the wood in its normal state before treatment. Another result was the elimination of virtually all complex jointing in the construction, as elements could be lapped over one another and joined with screws.

The armless side chair, introduced in 1876, was chosen by Adolf Loos for use in his buildings. Le Corbusier, however, selected the armchair, and the two architects were said to have had an argument in which each accused the other of having chosen the wrong one. The side chair has certainly been the more extensively mass-produced, in fact by 1900 about 40,000,000 had been manufactured.

The beautiful curves of the Thonet chairs, dictated by the intrinsic qualities of the material, were echoed by the Art Nouveau movement in which the same plant-like curves were used; but Thonet preceded the Art Nouveau style by some forty years. Bentwood had been used since the 18th century for the backs of rural, craft-built chairs — typically the Windsor type — but only a rather

Armless chair.

strained and gradual curve was possible before Thonet's process. The patents ran out a few years ago on the original patterns, and now there are several manufacturers copying the designs and developing others which employ the same principles. There are certain tubular metal chairs, for instance the Armchair 12 by Poul Kjaerholm (p. 138), that owe something to the general configuration of a Thonet chair, partly because the similar diameter and visual weight of the two materials dictate similarly appropriate curves. The Thonet chair uses wood expressively in its most natural-looking form, invoking the way it originally appears in trees — as a springy, pliant material supporting its load without resort to bulk and without strengthening joints. These chairs have been so widely distributed and have become so much part of our lives that it is difficult to judge them objectively. However, one can safely say that they are among the most beautiful man-made objects in our environment, and that familiarity never seems to detract from their appeal.

14

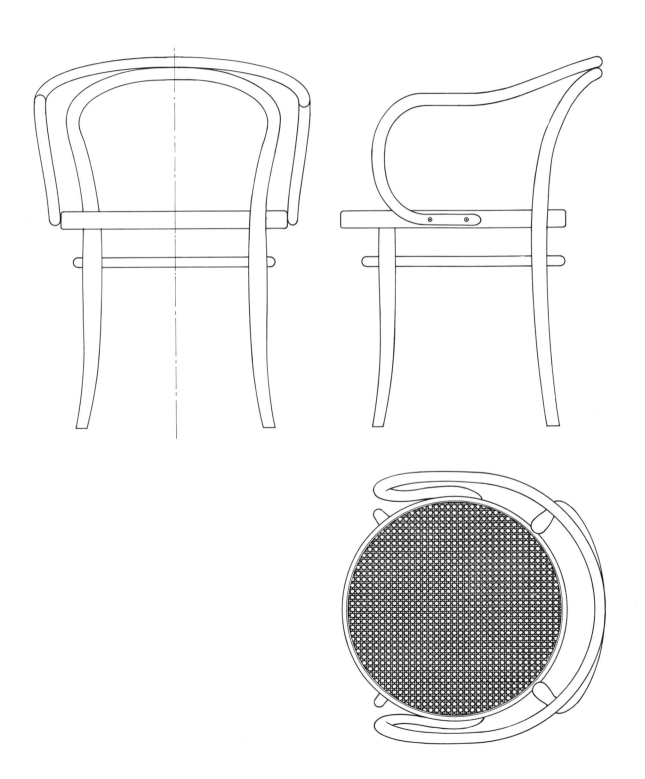

Colonial chair
Designer unknown
Mid-nineteenth century

This chair was originally designed to be used by British army officers in India. They needed a chair that was light in weight, could be folded up and carried around easily, could be used on uneven terrain without breaking and was reasonably comfortable. This was achieved by constructing the chair from a series of turned oak parts which were fitted into each other loosely and were not glued, being held together by a combination of leather straps and leather or canvas seat and back. The straps, arms, seat and back all acted under tension to keep the structure in place, while allowing it to adjust to uneven ground. The Colonial chair had no significant antecedents except early peasant rush seats which used round rods as stretchers which fitted into holes in the legs. The two classic derivations from this chair are Marcel Breuer's Wassily chair of 1925 (p. 41) and Le Corbusier's Basculant chair of 1928 (p. 61).

There are many variations on this chair made in different parts of the world, but most look rather weak in comparison with the original. The Colonial chair looks what it is, a strong, functional, work-horse of a chair, capable of roughing it out of doors and virtually lasting for ever. All its elements express their function perfectly – they are simple and direct. All parts are constructed at right angles, the angle of the seat is made by stretching the canvas or leather from front to back on two bars which are mounted at different heights, and the backrest is arranged on two pivoted strips of wood. All in all a very satisfying chair to look at, if not totally satisfying to sit in.

18

The design of these chairs was probably influenced by the colonial chair (see pages 40 and 60).

Wassily chair by
Marcel Breuer

The Basculant by
Le Corbusier

Tripolina
Joseph Beverly Fenby
England, 1877

This design was patented by Joseph Fenby, an inventor, in 1877. The chair was later manufactured in Italy as the Tripolina, and in the United States as the Gold Medal No. 4. This is a prototype from which a number of similar designs have sprung, notably the Hardoy chair designed in 1940 by the Argentinian architects Antonio Bonet, Juan Kurchan and Ferrari Hardoy.

The Tripolina's popularity with circus clowns and army officers on campaigns stems from its unsurpassed collapsibility — setting it up involves simply pulling it open and draping it with its seat/back sling. It is interesting that Fenby regarded his chair as an afterthought, and a stool with the same structure as having been his important invention, even though the traditional artist's tripod stool does the same job with only three pieces of wood and one connector. After a laborious description of the stool, Fenby's original patent refers to the chair as follows: 'For a camp chair four of the bars are made of an additional length so as to serve as a support for the back of the sitter.'

The earliest evidence of the chair's production in any great quantity is in 1895 when Gold Medal of Wisconsin began to make it. Apparently Fenby sold the rights to French and Italian manufacturers at about the same time. Although it is not as refined as later developments of the same structure, Fenby's design is still sufficiently slim and light to be a most economical lounge chair in terms of shape and materials. Moreover, its horizontal side members make it certainly more comfortable than the Hardoy, and easier to get out of.

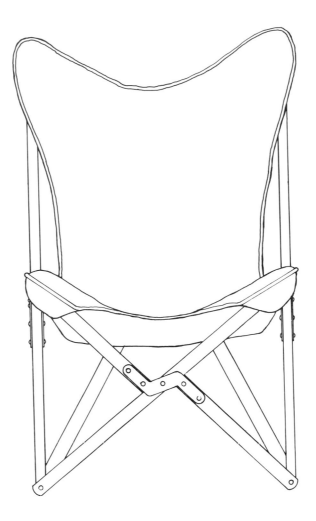

The AA chair, designed by Bonet, Ferrari and Hardoy (also called the Hardoy chair), U.S.A., 1938. Originally made by Knoll, U.S.A., this design is probably derived from the Italian campaign chair and the Tripolina, but uses a metal frame with V shaped legs over which the leather sling is fitted.

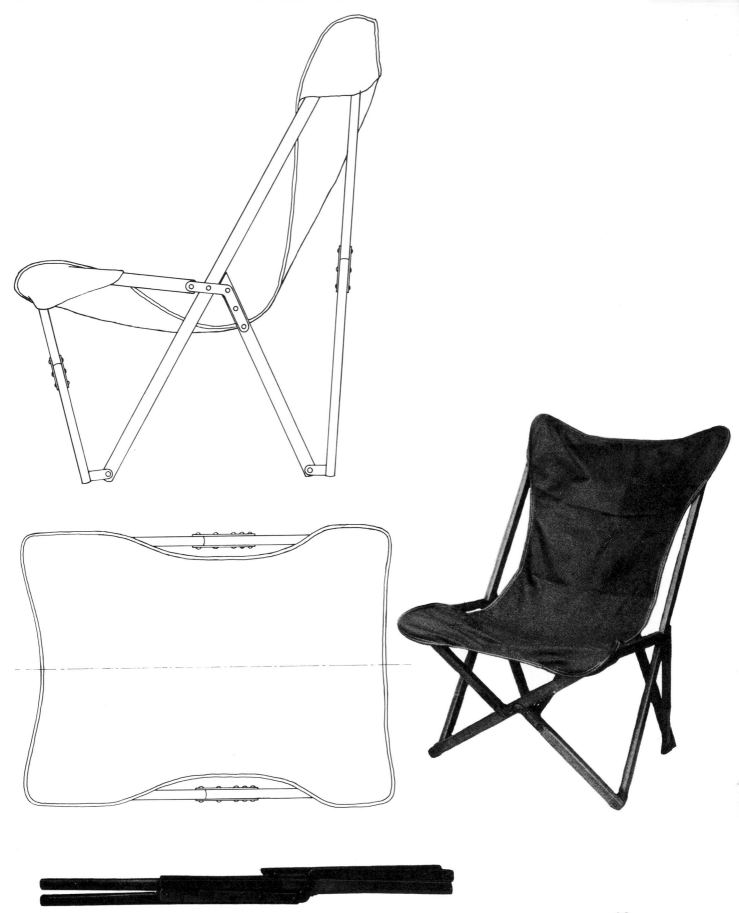

The Tripolina folds
compactly, the dog-legged
frame fitting flat when
closed.

23

Riemerschmid chair
Richard Riemerschmid
Germany, 1899

By the end of the nineteenth century the Arts and Crafts movement, and in particular William Morris, had revived simple, country-made chair forms, and brought about a taste for sophisticated but traditional forms. This chair, designed within the Art Nouveau idiom, follows Morris in its straightforward design and its return to classic chair forms, like those of the late eighteenth century, but it has far greater urbanity and polish. The chair was adapted and detailed by Edward Wormley in 1947, for the Dunbar Corporation. Riemerschmid himself approved the slight modifications to the chair, and complimented Wormley on his 'improvements in its form and comfort'.

The chair was originally designed for the Dresden Exhibition of 1899. Richard Riemerschmid belonged to the Munich group which was part of the Jugendstijl movement. This chair was one of his less flamboyant designs, although it clearly reflects the characteristic Art Nouveau feeling for natural growing forms, especially in such details as the flow of the arms into the back. The proportioning is beautifully worked out and even now the chair does not look dated.

Some of the more subtle construction details include the stepped-up thickening (for strength) of the side stretcher where it joins the back leg, and the way the armrests are laid on top of the supporting element, overlapping it by a small fraction and forming along the outer edge a thin line that flows up into the backrest. The Riemerschmid was created at the watershed of two quite distinct developments in design — those of Scandinavia and of Germany. It spans both traditions, and chairs which owe something to it can be seen in both groups. Richard Riemerschmid was an architect, and a designer of fabrics, glass and silverware, but he is mostly remembered for his furniture design. His contemporary, the architect van der Velde once said of him that 'each of his works is a good deed'.

26

This Riemerschmid chair, designed in the same year, shows a more original though less satisfying approach to structure. The diagonal brace triangulates both front and back legs and flows into the backrest with a typical but slightly dated Art Nouveau line.

Folding chair
Anonymous Sailor

c. 1905

This uncomfortable-looking chair is actually genuinely supportive in an un-expected way. The seat and back work like a pair of well-placed slings in which one sort of hangs in complete comfort and security. It is probably the smallest really comfortable chair ever designed and it was not even done by a designer, which may explain its totally unconventional approach to sup-porting the human body. It is also a very portable chair because it packs into the backrest, which is also a carrying bag.

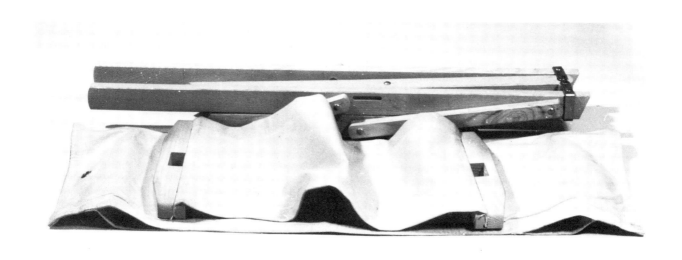

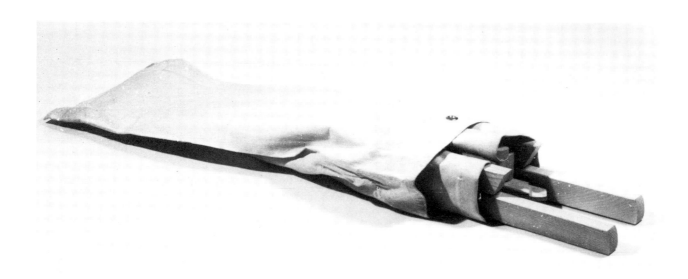

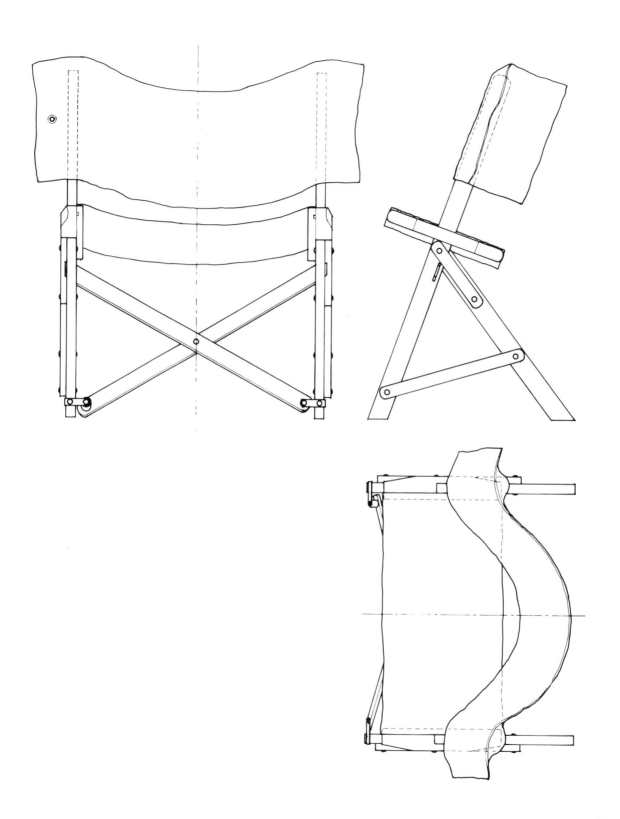

Red-Blue chair

Gerrit Rietveld

Holland, 1918

Gerrit Rietveld belonged to the De Stijl movement between 1919 and 1931. The chief spokesman for this group of artists was the painter Piet Mondrian, who described their theories as an attempt to close the gap between art and life. Their essential principle was that there should be purity of all elements; purity of unimpeded horizontals and verticals, and primary colours with black, white and grey. The paintings of Mondrian's mature style which have so many similarities to the Red-Blue chair began to emerge about two years after the chair was designed, implying an exchange of influences and ideas. The Red-Blue was not in fact originally painted at all, but Rietveld included it in the Schroder House, where it was to be seen against very dark walls and a dark

floor, which would have had a marvellous dematerializing effect on the structure as it is now painted.

The basic structure of the chair is black-stained bars which pass each other at right angles. These linear elements support two angled plywood planes, the back painted red and the seat blue. Rietveld's declared intention was to design a chair which anyone could afford, consisting of simple machine-cut elements put together with dowels and glue, and which depended in no way on expensive craftsmanship. He later designed a chair made out of packing-case timber, to be delivered in pieces and assembled according to simple instructions, by the purchaser. In spite of Rietveld's far-sighted ideas about the simplification and cost reduction of furniture making, the Red-Blue appears to be made solely according to aesthetic criteria, almost a sculpture or an architectural exercise: the functional aspect appears incidental. Rietveld himself is said to have complained of bruising his ankles on it, and a certain daring seems required actually to use the chair. The construction itself is very direct, and well adapted to mass-production.

Its dimensions are all based on a ten-centimetre module, so that the chair can be made without using complex working drawings. The colouring is also completely straightforward. The black-stained bars have bright yellow ends, which, as they are square or squatly rectangular, read as small planes. Against the dark floor, the chair would be seen as two large primary coloured planes surrounded by a multiplicity of small ones shimmering in space.

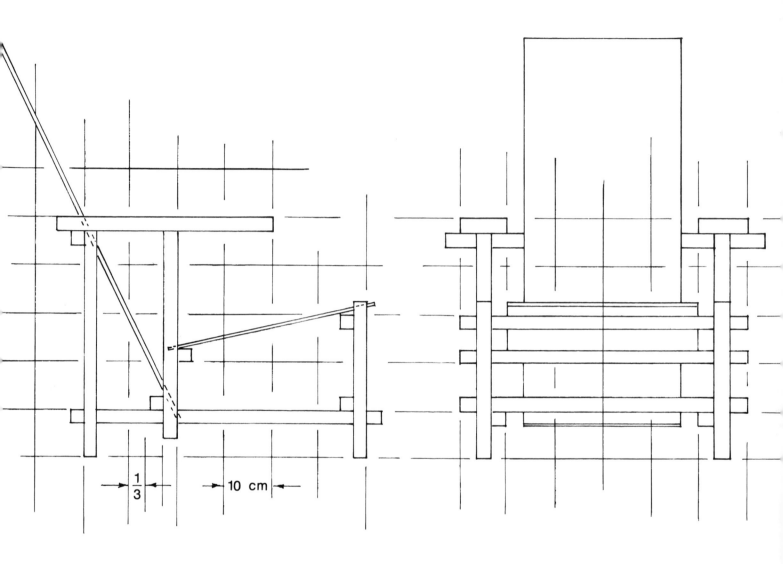

$\dfrac{1}{3}$ 10 cm

The Berlin chair
Gerrit Rietveld
Holland, 1923

In 1923 Rietveld and the De Stijl painter, Huszar, designed a model room for an exhibition in Berlin, Huszar planning the colour and Rietveld the furniture and layout. The Berlin chair was designed for this exhibit.

Rietveld has sacrificed anatomical considerations in order to produce what is virtually a De Stijl sculpture in an unlimited edition, with all the characteristic juxtaposition of planes in space and subtle differentiation of parts using various greys. It is strongly reminiscent of Mondrian's earlier paintings. The Berlin chair is unlike the Red-Blue both in its asymmetry and the predominance of planes rather than lines.

Structurally, all the parts add rigidity to each other, rendering the simple lapped joins perfectly strong.

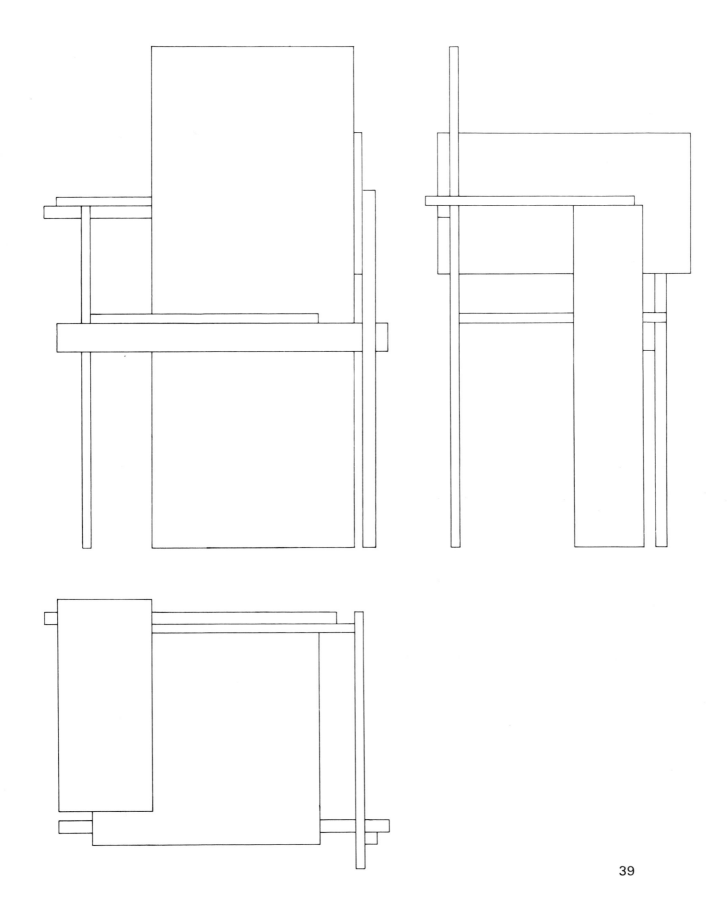

Wassily chair

Marcel Breuer

Germany, 1925

Named after the painter Wassily Kandinsky, for whose home at the Bauhaus it was made, the Wassily has a most complex arrangement of parts, with thin strip-like planes intersecting and by-passing each other at various levels, supported by a broad tubular steel frame which describes in a fine shiny line the shape of a well-proportioned, stable armchair. This creates an effect of strength which is in fact borne out by the structure itself. The chair is visually very satisfying, and its rather intricate design works beautifully. The casual way in which the steel elements overlap and are bolted together at their connecting points is unique, and, together with the complexity of the structure, is probably a product of Breuer's pioneering attempts to use tubular metal to its full potential. He was primarily interested in finding out the possibilities offered by the use of such a visually fine material, and did not only use it for its strength. The legend runs that he was inspired to use tubular metal for furniture after contemplating the handlebars of a bicycle. Le Corbusier's swivel-backed Basculant chair (p. 61) is superficially similar, but makes an illuminating comparison with the Wassily, which is so much less straightforward in construction. One can indeed say, in paraphrase of it's designer's famous dictum, that the Basculant is a machine for sitting in. The Wassily, however, could never be so described. It is a welcoming and a beautiful chair, both aesthetically and physically satisfying.

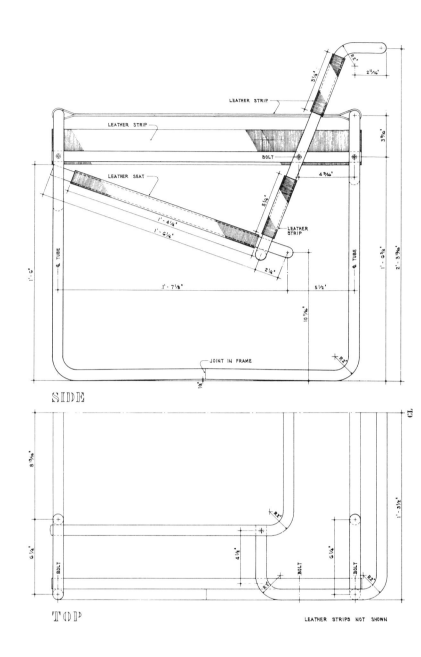

SIDE

TOP

LEATHER STRIPS NOT SHOWN

Detail of the Wassily chair, showing the frame's structure. The parts of the frame are screwed to one another, the main pieces being joined half way along the floor bars. The leather is seamed in loops over the supporting elements, and the whole chair has a degree of flexibility, that increases slightly as the leather loosens with wear.

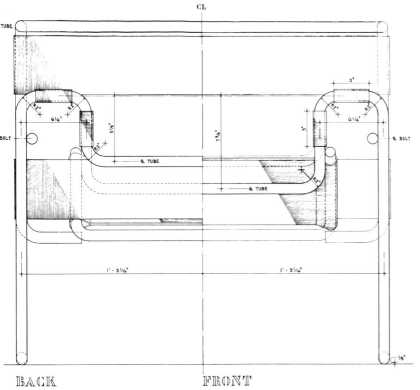

BACK   FRONT

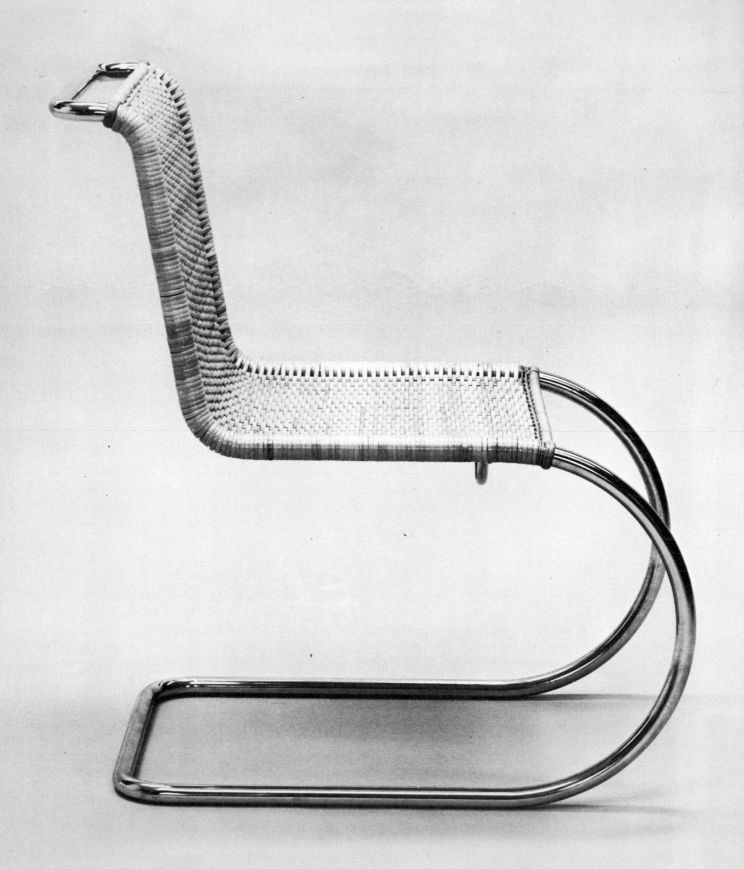

MR chair
Mies van der Rohe
Germany, 1926

This chair was designed at the time of the earliest use of the cantilever principle for metal-frame chairs. In this case the cantilever is directly expressed by the use of a half-circle at the front, acting as a curved spring. Even though all the lines in this chair are strictly geometric — a series of straight lines and half and quarter circles — the impression it gives is of a very graceful, springy, flowing form. The idea of the continuous line of side support becoming the base element along the floor, had a very far-reaching influence. In fact we have seen so many similar uses of tubular steel that it is difficult to appreciate the sophistication of this beautiful chair.

The MR was originally produced with a continuous seat and back of woven cane, either lacquered black or left its natural colour. Alternatively it was made with separate seat and back of leather, held in place with metal strips and bolts. This fixing was later modified to a complete wrap-around leather cover, laced together at the back. A version of the chair with arms was also made originally, which gave the chair the appearance of a closer connection to the Thonet rocking-chair shape. The arms curved from the back to join the main curve below its outermost point, and they accentuated the airy suppleness of the structure. The armed version seems much less stark, though the arms are un-mistakably afterthoughts, and are not entirely satisfactorily connected to the main structure.

An original production model of the MR chair. (The metal has been painted at a later date.) Originally, the chair was offered with either leather or cane seat/back.
In the collection of the Victoria and Albert Museum, London.

The current production model of the MR chair with leather seat and back The lacing of the leather at the back and below the seat allows adjustment of the tension. It is still available in cane.

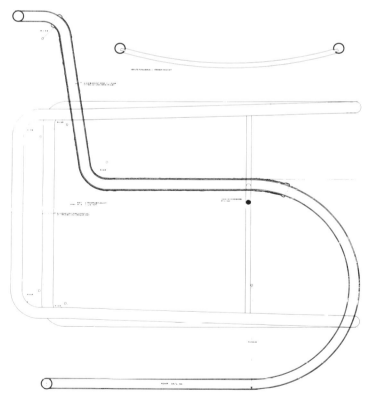

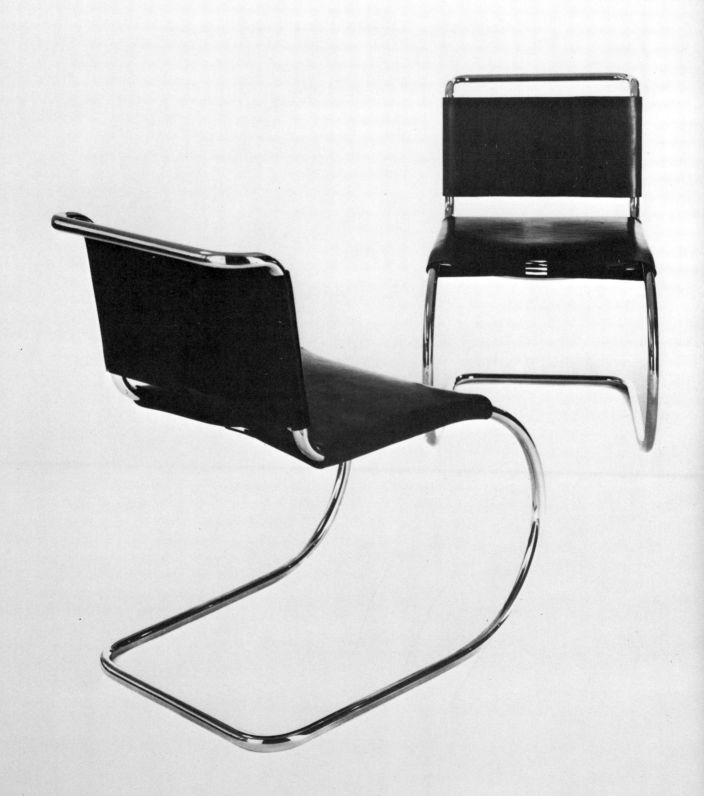

Tatlin chair
Vladimir Tatlin
U.S.S.R., 1927

Vladimir Tatlin was a leader of the Russian Constructivist movement, and the Tatlin is the only existing chair from this period. The example shown here is, as far as I know, the only production model since Tatlin's own prototype. It differs from the original in that the frame has been made in steel instead of bent wood, because of the apparent impossibility of producing a wood frame of sufficient soundness. Tatlin was deeply involved in the making of flying machines. He created great winged forms made out of literally bentwood skeletons, covered in canvas and occasionally reinforced with whalebone. His structures stretched the tensile and loadbearing capacities of the wood to the utmost, and clearly this chair is an adaptation of the principle learnt for these primitive exercises in aerodynamics — the flow of stress through load-bearing members from tight grouping to a wide splay.

In the bentwood prototype, the points where the lines met — on the ground and half way up the back — were bound with cane. In the present model there are single screws visible at each of these points. The only other change from the original structure is the tightening of the curve where the back leg tube leaves the floor. This makes the legs more vertical and considerably less graceful.

The seat is a quite distinct unit, placed within the structural web of this linear chair. It is a modified tractor saddle with contoured padding and an intricately tailored leather covering, and is beautiful in its own right. This remains a most elegant chair, and shows no sign of looking dated after the almost half century between conception and production, though the present model is not quite the graceful, swooping, organic form that Tatlin originally designed.

The original Tatlin chair, made in the same way that Tatlin built his flying contraptions, with bent wood, bound by split cane, supporting a simple seat element.

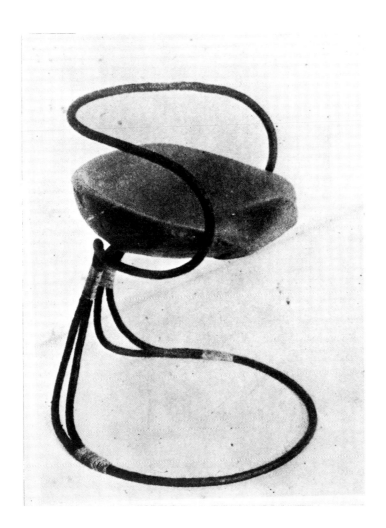

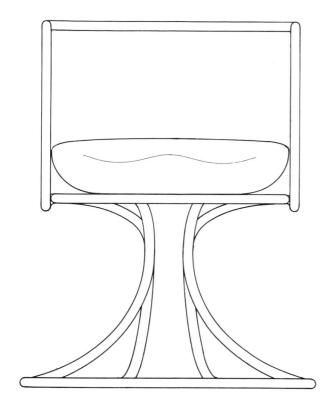

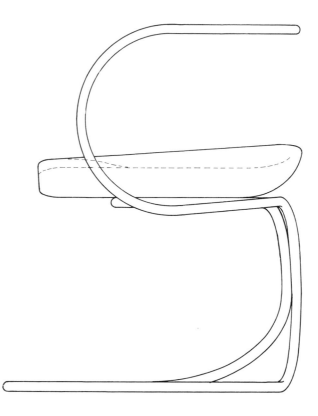

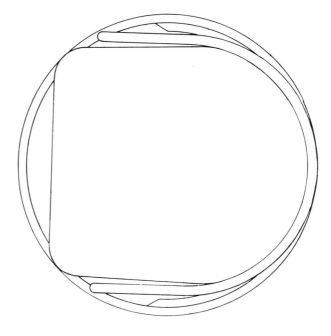

Cesca
Marcel Breuer
Germany, 1928

Like the MR the Cesca was designed on the cantilever principle which was capturing the imagination of architects and engineers at the time and was subsequently to appear in many more furniture designs. The Cesca still remains the most perfectly resolved use of the cantilever with its elegantly formed wood stretchers for the caned seat and back and the added cantilever of the arm version. Breuer, who had designed several non cantilever chairs and tables, got the idea for the Cesca from seeing one of his tables on its side. Mart Stam who was in contact with Breuer at the time realised what Breuer had in mind and managed to put together elements of an existing Breuer chair and table to make a crudely designed predecessor to the Cesca. Thonet have recently applied all the proportions and angles of the Cesca to Stam's chair and are marketing the resultant hybrid as a Stam design!

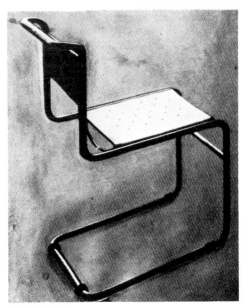

Cantilever chair by Mart Stam, designed in Germany in 1926, now made by Gebrüder Thonet. Stam was aware of Breuer's work on cantilevers, and made this steel chair before Breuer himself took up his own idea in the design of the Cesca. The production model of the Stam chair has what is virtually a Breuer frame with leather surfaces. All its angles and proportions are Breuer's.

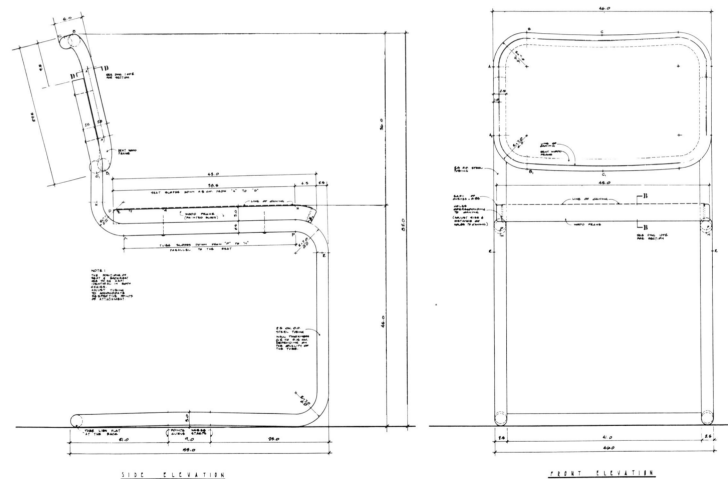

SIDE ELEVATION

FRONT ELEVATION

PARTIAL PLAN

Other views of the Cesca chair showing the adaptation of the flow of line from the cantilever into the arm rests with only a small outward deflection of the steel tube.

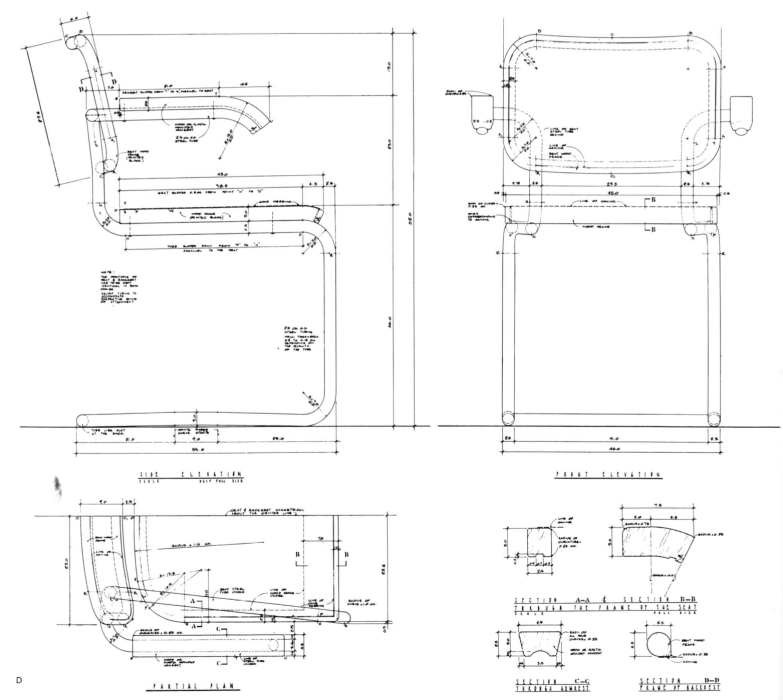

SIDE ELEVATION
SCALE HALF FULL SIZE

FRONT ELEVATION

PARTIAL PLAN

SECTION A-A & SECTION B-B
THROUGH THE FRAME OF THE SEAT
FULL SIZE

SECTION C-C
THROUGH ARMREST

SECTION D-D
FRAME OF BACKREST

D

Lounge chair
Marcel Breuer
Germany, 1928

Breuer's lounge chair is directly related to his Cesca chair in the shaping of the tubular frame and the wooden armrests. On the other hand the cane-seat construction is closer to Mies van der Rohe's MR chair. This chair was only produced for ten years and put back into production in 1970.

Photo: Peter Paige

This leather version of the 1928 lounge chair is
less satisfactory because the leather follows the
line of the frame in a slightly awkward manner.

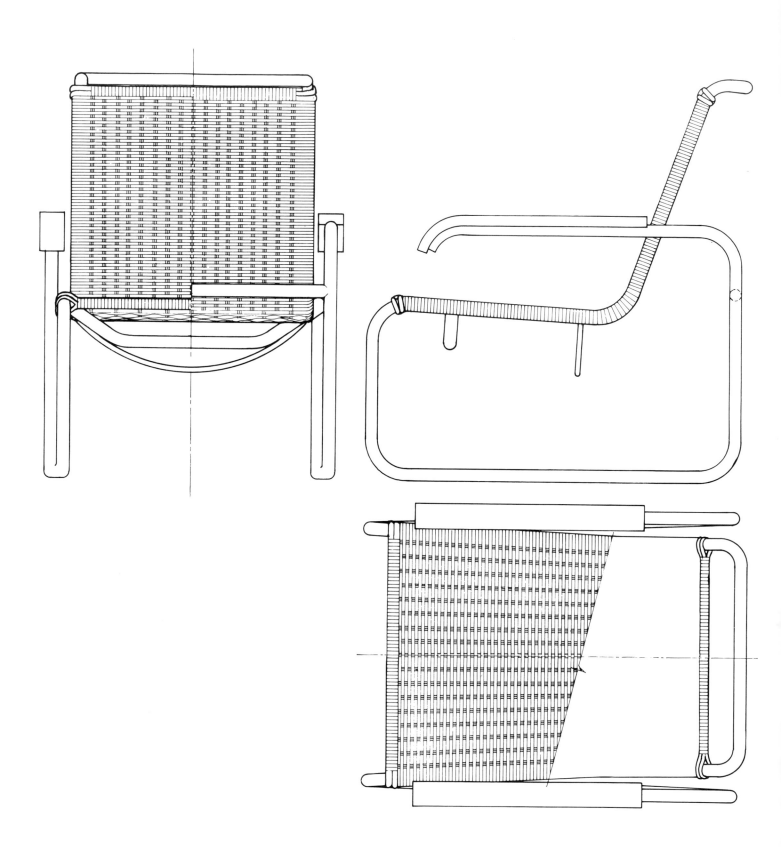

Basculant

Le Corbusier

France, 1928

The Basculant has a frame of chromium-nickel-plated tubular steel, with calf-skin seat and back, and leather strap arm rests. For the interiors of his own buildings, Le Corbusier originally chose chairs and other objects that he thought were so 'mass produced' as to be virtually anonymous. But later he and his office, notably Charlotte Perriand and Pierre Jeanneret, began to design furniture, of which this is one of the earliest examples. The Basculant appears to be in contrast with Le Corbusier's earlier idea, in that it has a comparatively complicated construction, and uses extravagant materials. The formula of pliable elements supported by a simple strong frame in this way is possibly derived from the chairs used by British Army Officers in India and other early campaign furniture, but the problems here have been resolved in a very different way.

The curved section of the side frame bending towards the back seems a perfectly logical structural support, avoiding an awkward stress-bearing corner joint behind the seat. This side section enhances the impression that the chair is slung between the supporting legs. The whole simple profile makes the Basculant look more flexible than it in fact is. The front elevation, with two lateral spacer bars, beautifully clear verticals and long smooth strap arms ranged round the accommodating calf-skin seat and back, gives the impression of sturdiness, and, despite the chair's small scale, of a very spacious structure.

The seat and back membranes are held under tension by a series of springs, and the back is pivoted to allow freedom of posture, from a slouch to an upright position.

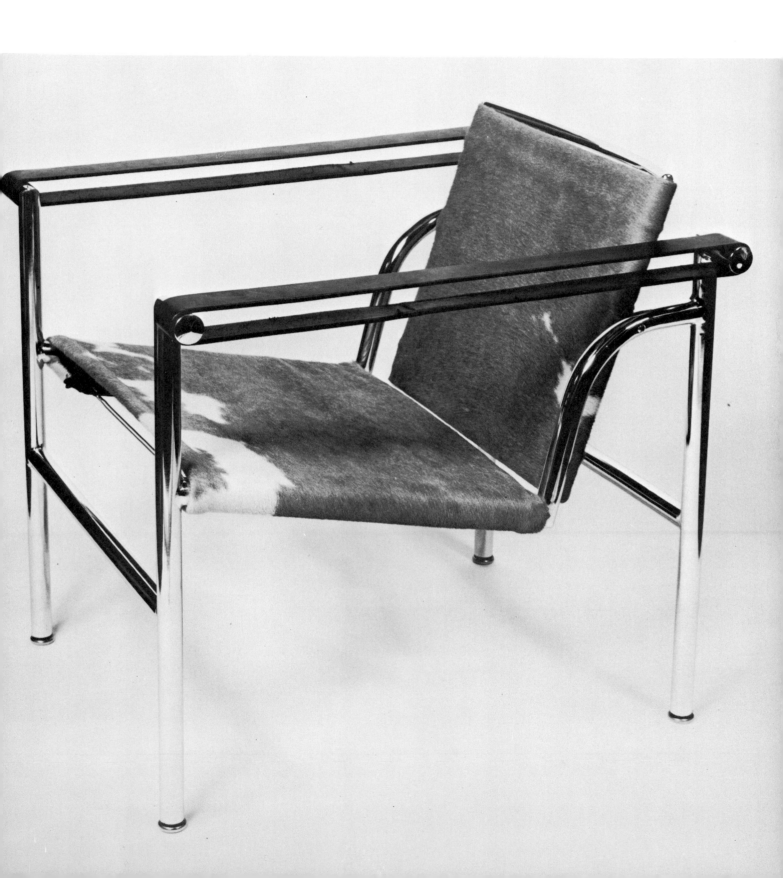

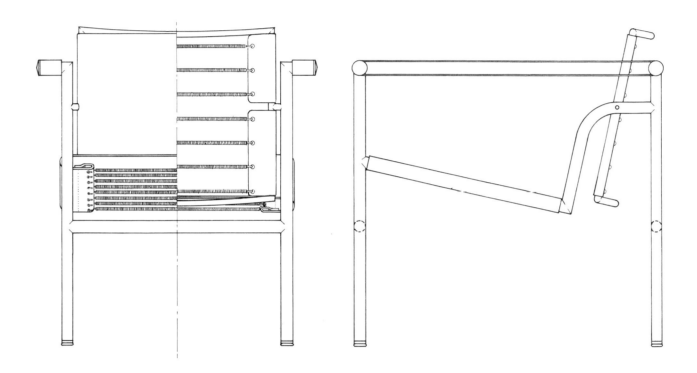

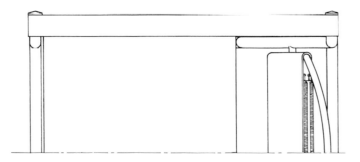

The calfskin seat and back elements of the Basculant are held under tension by a row of steel springs, over the frame which is itself held in tension by bow pieces. The arm straps are simply looped over the turned tops of the leg tubes, with a small flange to retain them.

Chaise longue

Le Corbusier
France, 1928

Designed by Le Corbusier in association with his partner, Charlotte Periand, and used in the furnishing of his Villa d'Avray, this is the first chaise to be made adjustable by simply moving the whole seat element within its quite separate support frame. The seat is padded pony skin, supported by steel tension springs on a shallow curve of chromium-plated tubular steel. The seat is shaped in three planes, following the line of a flexed body and legs, lapping over the frame at either end, and it lies on the smooth curve of the underside, which is in turn supported by two thick rubber-covered lateral bars on a rigid steel base. The rubber covering allows the seat to be placed at any angle on the two bars, from flat to almost upright, tilted either way, without slipping when you sit on it. This chaise, with its three contrasting surfaces — pony-skin, chromium-plating and matt-textured steel, and its leather head pad and straps, seems an elaborate construction, even for a total relaxation chair. But, when you have adjusted the angle to get your feet at a satisfactory level above your head, and settled the position of the head cushion exactly, you find that it is truly one of the classics for complete rather egocentric comfort.

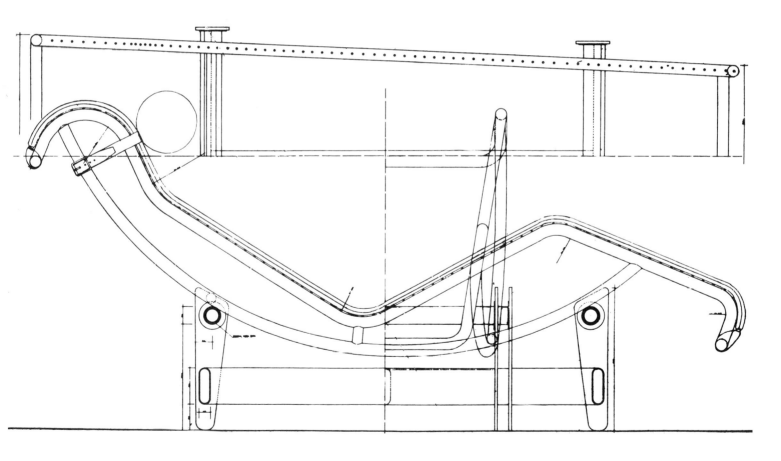

Chaise longue by Poul Kjaerholm for comparison.

Grand Confort

Le Corbusier

France, 1928

An offshoot of the long family tree of overstuffed chairs, the Grand Confort is composed of four large loose cushions fitting within a basket-like frame which holds them in their respective positions as arms, back and seat. The frame is made of chromium-nickel-plated tubular steel with a wire mesh across to support the seat cushion. The chair's actual seat space is small, giving the sitter a feeling of being held. It was designed on a cube principle, with the intention of making a chair whose structure was plainly declared, rather than buried inside upholstery. The Grand Confort has complete clarity of design, and is a highly original solution to the problem of real comfort. It can be seen to have influenced many recent designers of ultra-comfortable armchairs and sofas, notably Mario Bellini, with his 1967 design consisting of big cushions held in relationship simply by a broad strap, slotted as a belt is slotted, through flat retaining loops (p. 162). The external structure means that the upholstered elements are no more than they appear to be, and they are so designed that they do not need to be fixed in position. This idea of freely arranged upholstery has become popular lately, with various types of joined cushions forming flexible seating elements with and without a supporting structure. Indeed, Le Corbusier's ideas, with a radical new architectural logic manifested in methodically developed designs, produced many of the basic principles which showed today's designers the way towards 'free form' in furniture. He, more than any of the twentieth century pioneers of chair design, took the problem back to its most elemental stage, and re-thought the existing structural conventions.

A rarity in the design of metal furniture is the use of frame elements varying in section according to their function. The bar running around the cushions halfway up the frame is very thin, because it simply works as a tension member,

whereas the heavier top bar is actually a structural element connecting the legs. The frame below the seat is an L section, holding the mesh and making a tray in which the seat cushion firmly fits, wedged by the three vertical cushions sitting in the same tray on their edges. Instead of bending the tubular steel, Le Corbusier welded the corners where the sections of tube join, and ground them to an acute curve.

There is a wider version of this chair, which deviates from the original cube shape to give a more generous proportion. It seems more conventional in feeling, and unnecessarily large, considering the comfort of the cube version — a comfort that is unusual in such a small arm-chair.

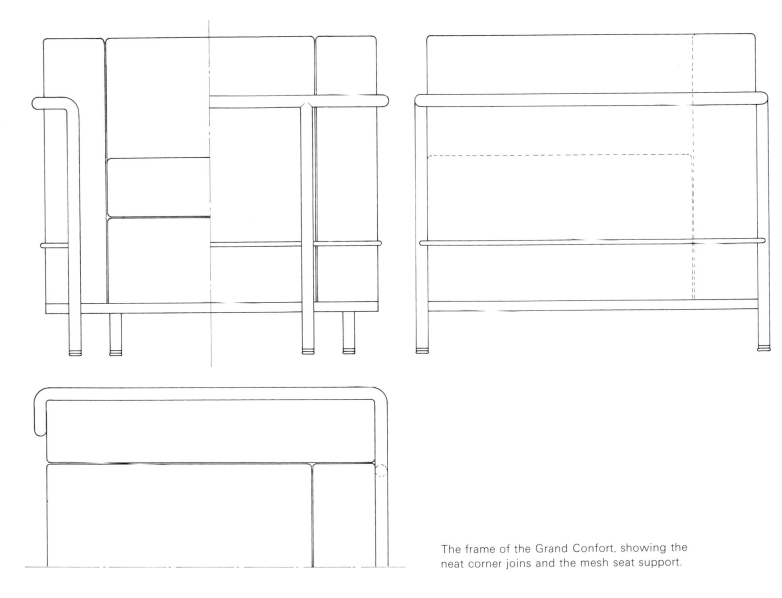

The frame of the Grand Confort, showing the neat corner joins and the mesh seat support.

Barcelona chair

Mies van der Rohe

Germany, 1929

This chair was designed by Mies van der Rohe for the German Government pavilion, which he designed for the Barcelona International Exhibition of 1929. The brief was to design a chair fit to receive a king, a dictator or an ambassador — it was to be a very important chair. The design succeeds in matching and conferring dignity — the Barcelona is elegant, costly and monumental.

The amount of hand work required in the making of this chair is staggering. The upholstery is composed of forty separately cut panels joined by narrow hand-sewn welts; the leather straps are held on by seventy-two screws each tapped and screwed into the metal frame through the ends of the straps; the stainless steel frame is all electric arc welded, hand finished, and polished to a perfect mirror finish. Apart from some machine sewing and the extruded-steel sections the chair is almost entirely hand-made, which explains its high purchase price. In spite of all this, the finished chair could never be said to emphasise, nor even to reveal its own production methods, nor has it any trace of 'hand-made by craftsmen' connotations.

There have been several modifications in the production since the original design. The chromed steel has been replaced by polished stainless steel, and the cotton, burlap and horsehair filling of the upholstery has been superceded by foam rubber. This has resulted in an even more long lasting chair, with virtually nothing to wear out.

The Barcelona is a fine chair, and has a marvellously generous scale. The solid metal section of the double X shaped frame makes it a very heavy chair, a fact belied by the visual effect of its beautiful formal balance.

Mies van der Rohe's approach here has been likened to gothic architecture, with its cathedral-like skeletons of exposed, flowing, linear structures. In his

own architecture, however, the structure is purely rectilinear, but the details are worked out with a finesse that is indeed comparable to gothic stone detailing. (This is particularly apparent in buildings such as Farnworth House, Crown Hall, the Institute of Technology of Chicago, and the new National Gallery of Berlin.)

The Barcelona chair is at its best in an open space, where it can be appreciated from a distance away, or where it can be seen from a low angle.

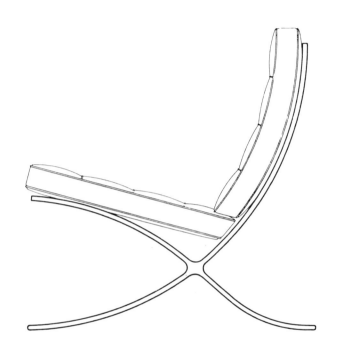

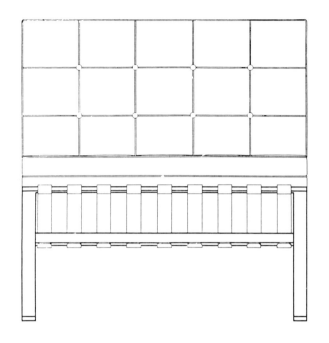

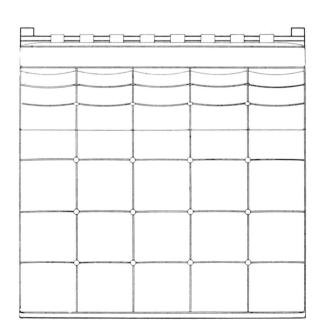

Tugendhat chair
Mies van der Rohe
Germany, 1929

This chair was designed, like the Brno (p. 80), for the Tugendhat House. It uses a seat/back construction closely similar to the Barcelona (p. 73), the flat, rectangular cushions lie on leather straps looped over a solid section steel frame. The support element is a cantilever, and the complete frame is a clear expression of its function at every point. In contrast, the Barcelona frame is structurally ambiguous; the steel is used to create a prestigious and elegant design, whose roots are in aesthetic, rather than functional considerations.

As in both the Barcelona and the Brno, a flat steel strip is used for the frame of the Tugendhat. The flat metal has an appearance of malleability in its bent state, that is absent from the more stark and definitive statement of the curves in the MR, for instance, where tube is used (p. 44).

The Tugendhat has a similar sled-like look of sturdy streamlining as Poul Kjaerholm's Chair 20 (p. 166), but the flat floor bar effectively finalizes the balance of the design. Also the Tugendhat's S shaped double-curved supports emphasize the difference in proportion between the light cantilever element and the upholstery. This is in contrast with Kjaerholm's design, where a fine seat element appears poised on a broad, strong frame.

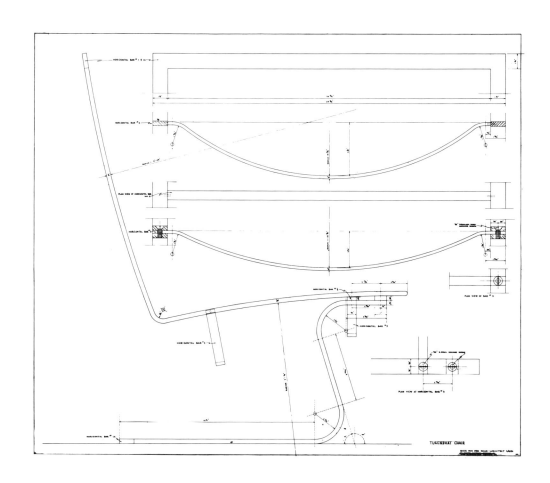

TUGENDHAT CHAIR

Brno chair
Mies van der Rohe
Germany, 1930

This chair was designed for the Tugendhat House in Brno, Czechoslovakia. Much greater strength is achieved in this design, visually and physically, by the use of flat metal sections for the frame, and the flat ground level spacer. The fact that the frame disappears behind the shallow upholstered elements, leaving the leg/arm lines the only visible support gives the chair a more cohesive form. The seat and back are firmly held in relation to one another, and relieved of any structural load. Like the Barcelona (p. 72), the chair is almost entirely hand made, though far fewer operations are required.

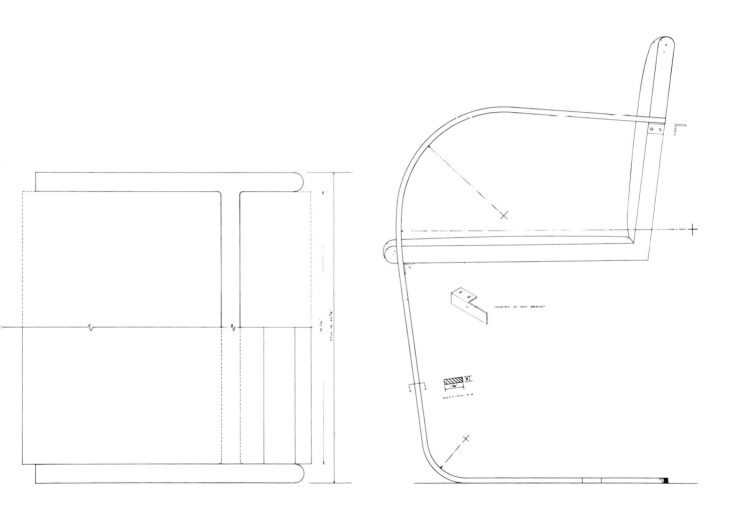

ISOMETRIC OF SEAT BRACKET

SECTION AA

Further views of the Brno
chair. These models show the
small arm pads that have been
recently added to the design.

Armchair 406
Alvar Aalto
Finland, 1933

This armchair, and others like it, stem from Aalto's Armchair 41, designed in 1930. Aalto was concerned with bent laminated and ply-wood, searching out its strengths in curves and in cantilever structures. He had designed a cantilever chair in 1930, using a formed plywood seat/back on a metal frame, but after three years of experimenting, during which he laminated and formed the wood himself in many variations, Aalto was able to get enough support from wood alone. His forms are springy and entirely natural and appropriate to the material, but his technique was highly sophisticated, and included the subtle extension of the number of laminations proportionately at points where extra load or stress had to be born. He developed a whole series of related designs using variations of his basic technique. The webbing seat membrane is another Aalto characteristic, taken up by other Scandinavian designers, notably Bruno Mathsson. Canvas or hemp used in this way gives that particularly attractive natural look to unpainted wooden furniture, and it makes a very comfortable and hard-wearing contact surface.

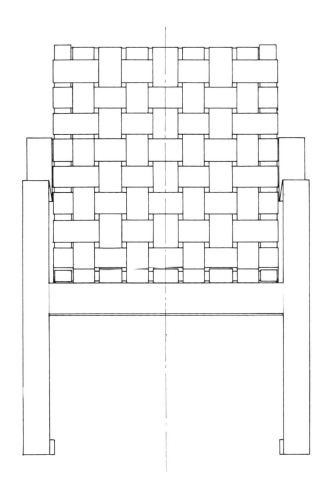

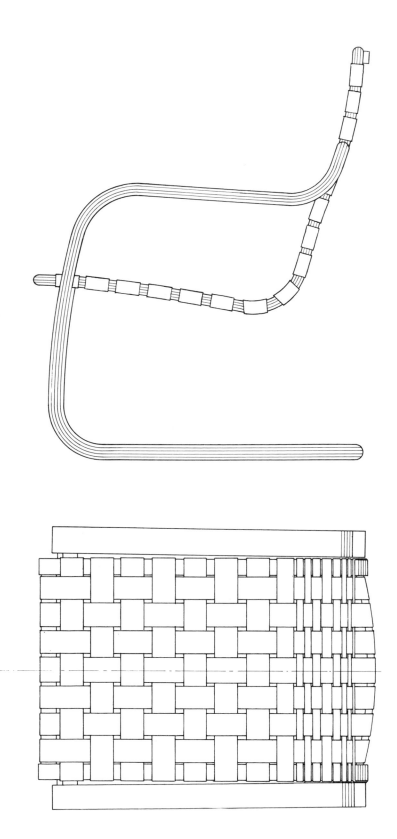

Easy chair 140.00
Ole Gjerløv-Knudson
Denmark, 1933

This chair is a study in the use of tension as a structural principle. A single compression strut under the seat opposes the tension of the seat plane, the top of the backrest, and the tourniquet, which creates all the other tensions. The idea for this chair was inspired by the traditional wood-framed bush saw, which uses an almost identical structure to tension the blade. The way in which the angle of the back is created by a transition from tension to looseness is simple, ingenious, and effective, resulting in the simplest and one of the most comfortable folding chairs in existence. It is also one of the few folding chairs with no metal parts.

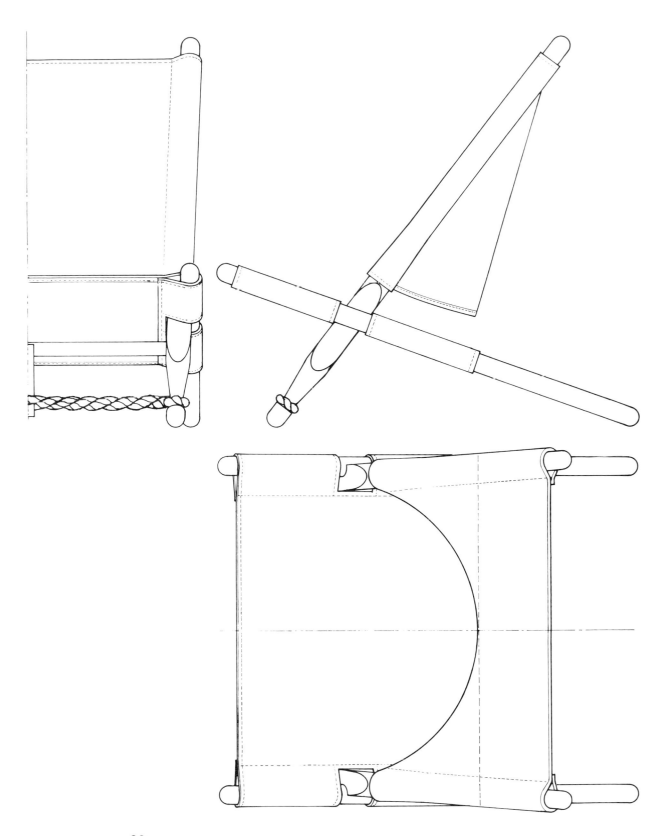

90

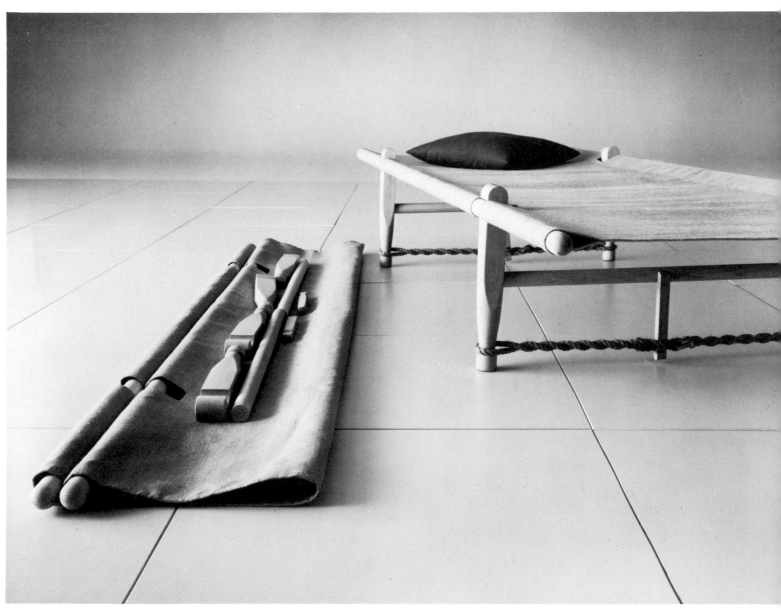

Stretcher bed, also by Ole Gjerløv-Knudson, using similar structure.

Zig-zag chair

Gerrit Rietveld

Holland, 1934

The Zig-zag chair is a stark assertion of function — a platform and support for the seated human frame. The reduction of the structure to four unobstructed and unadorned planes has engendered a whole range of new thoughts and possibilities, taken up by later designers, for the distribution of load-bearing members and the absorbtion of stress. The formal quality of the object itself has also been profoundly influential. To design a chair after coming in contact with the Zig-zag, one is in a way forced to start from a new point of departure, with a new initial premise, and to consider each line, plane, support or elaboration of chair structure using much more stringent criteria.

Rietveld's intention was to make a one-piece chair, but he was defeated by the material. Verner Panton's stacking chair (p. 130) has been compared to the Zig-zag, and it is clear that it embodied Rietveld's intention, though in a rather more relaxed form. Rietveld also intended the chair to use a minimum of room space. Though it is very arresting in isolation, the chair mixes surprisingly well with other furnishings. The Zig-zag is a small chair, and it appears poised, almost as if alert to its task, and ready to receive one's weight. I know a Zig-zag owner who willingly demonstrates the chair's strength by standing on the back edge, and though he may wobble, the chair will not shift. Although the construction is of extreme simplicity, the wood itself needs very specialized treatment. It is important that the beech wood be well seasoned, or the chair will be distorted quickly by warping: and this is especially ruinous if the foot becomes curved.

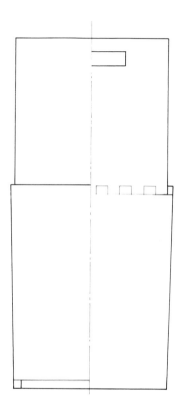

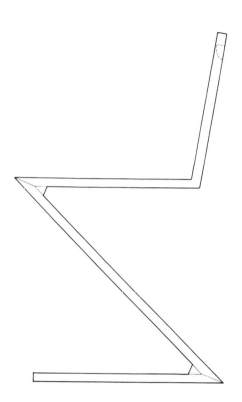

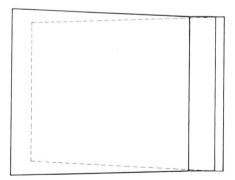

94

In making this chair of hardwood, only dovetail
joints are necessary, but in softwood these must be
reinforced with a batten and bolts. The chair has a
small hand-hold slot cut out of the back—a pleasing
detail in such a stark design.

Landi

Hans Coray
Switzerland, 1938

Designed as a stacking park chair for the Swiss National Exhibition in Zurich in 1938, the Landi used the latest developments of the time in aluminium technology, both in terms of alloys and hardening treatments. The shell is made for strength and flexibility whereas the leg structure is as rigid as possible. The shell is a single mass-produced shape, comparable to the Eames shell of eleven years later. The finish is slightly crystaline in appearance as a result of heat and chemical treatments required for the shell's physical properties. This finish is one of the most satisfactory possible on aluminium. There have been dozens of chairs quite obviously based on the Landi, and in many cases these are neater and slimmer and more shapely, but surprisingly most of them now look dated compared with their model — a testament to its underplayed styling and real concern with function and manufacturing suitability.

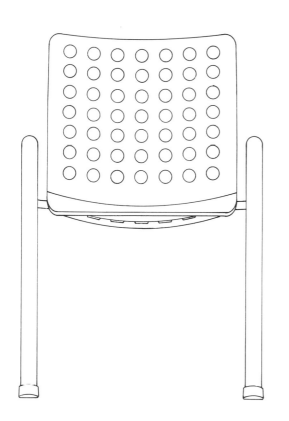

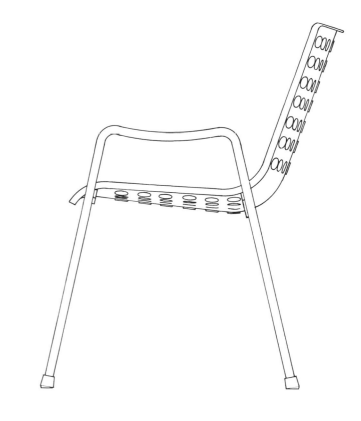

98

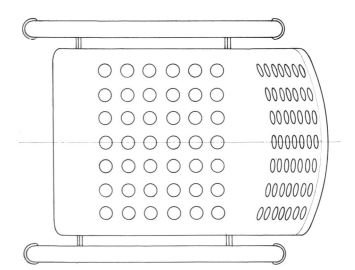

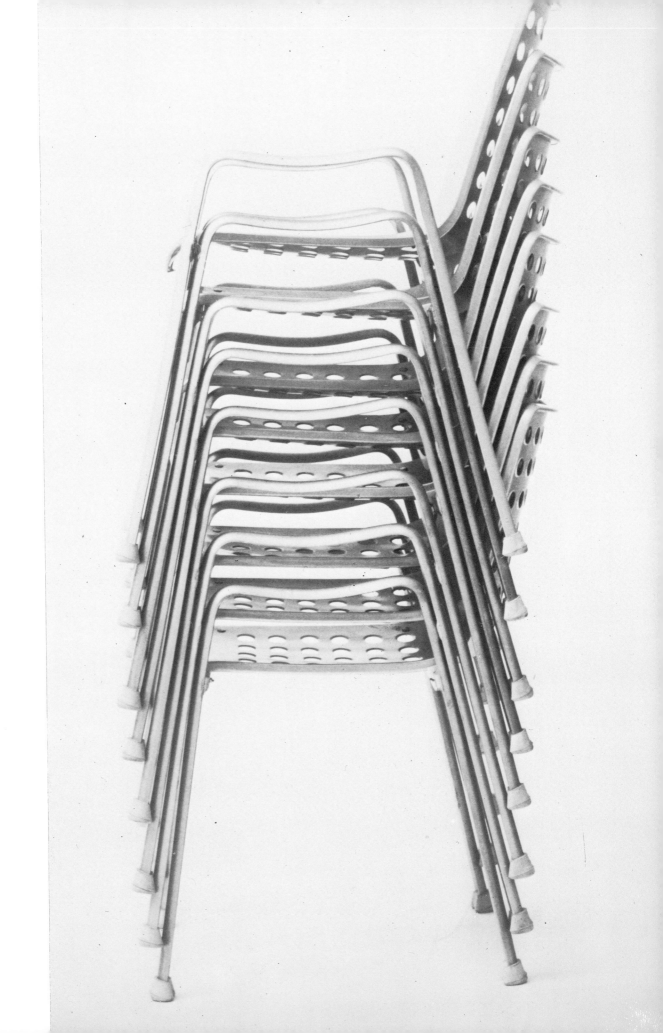

Part 2
The Post War Period

The classics described in the previous section laid the foundation for the developments to come. Eames' plastic shell designs could not have been made without the work on aluminium forming pioneered by Hans Coray. Poul Kjaerholm developed the use of steel which Mies van der Rohe and Breuer originated. Panton's plastic stacking chair is related to Rietveld's stackable Zig-zag chair, and Rowland's stacker is the ultimate refinement of the sort of technology which Coray started by using the latest metallurgy processes. Eames' uses of plywood are refinements of what Aalto began; Wegner owes much to Riemerschmid, and Bellini to Le Corbusier or more correctly to his brother Pierre Jeanneret and Charlotte Perriand.

The period is characterized by refinements of the classic ideas and by developments of their implications resulting from the availability of new materials and techniques.

LCM chair
Charles Eames
U.S.A., 1946

The LCM was, both technologically and in its design, an exceedingly advanced chair. Eames had been experimenting with formed plywood for a number of years (he was side-tracked during the war to the production of a leg splint for the United States Navy), and with the mechanics of joining different materials with a strong by flexible joint. The LCM is made in two leg heights, with a chromium-plated steel leg frame assembled with three electric resistance welds. This frame supports separate moulded-plywood seat and back panels. The chair is made in ash, walnut or birch, left natural or stained black or red. The legs were originally rubber tipped, but Eames substituted small self-levelling plastic feet. The thick circular rubber pad by which the elements are joined was used many times by Eames, and adapted and perfected in subsequent designs. The plywood panels are moulded to a very comfortable form, and the whole chair has an open aspect and a vital degree of flexibility.

Charles Eames collaborated with Eero Saarinen in the early forties, and they each later had an enormous influence on the development of furniture technology and design. To our eyes now, the LCM expresses the very best in post-war design. The structure stands undisguised, completely appropriate to the way people live in the mid-century period, and possessing an undeniable appeal.

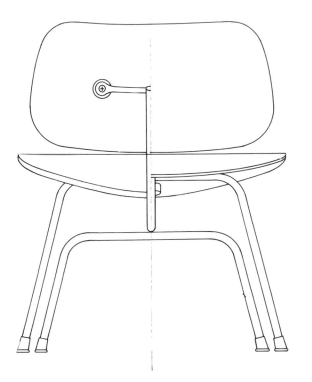

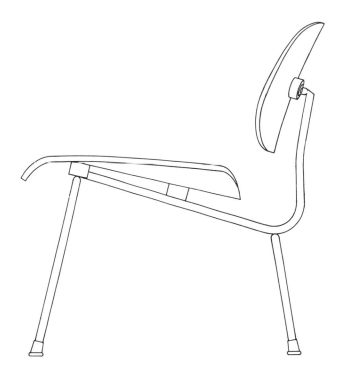

The pad by which the join is made between the frame and the plywood elements of the LCM chair. The screw connects with a nut embedded in the pad itself, and thus the metal element is easily fixed, through the round flattened disc at the end of the tubular frame.

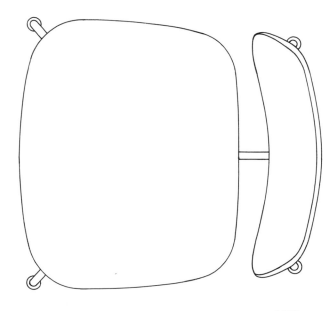

Barwa chaise

Edgar O. Bartolucci and Jack Waldheim
U.S.A., 1947

Unlike most of the chairs one would regard as classics, the Barwa has rather offhand detailing, but, considering its intended use as an outdoor chaise, its design seems appropriate. The V-shaped base is positioned and angled to enable the user to tip the chaise into a reclining position with a slight shift of body weight, an amazingly simple mechanism for changing the sitting angle. The removable canvas cover comes in some rather strident colors, which make the chair look somewhat less than classic, but this could be overcome if it were made available with an unbleached canvas and perhaps a black anodized frame.

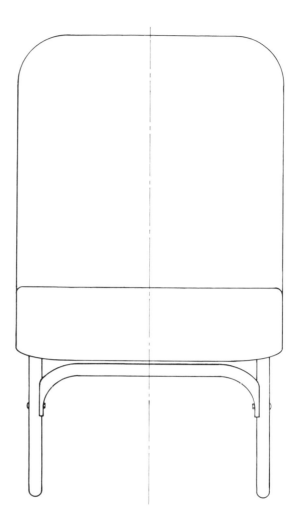

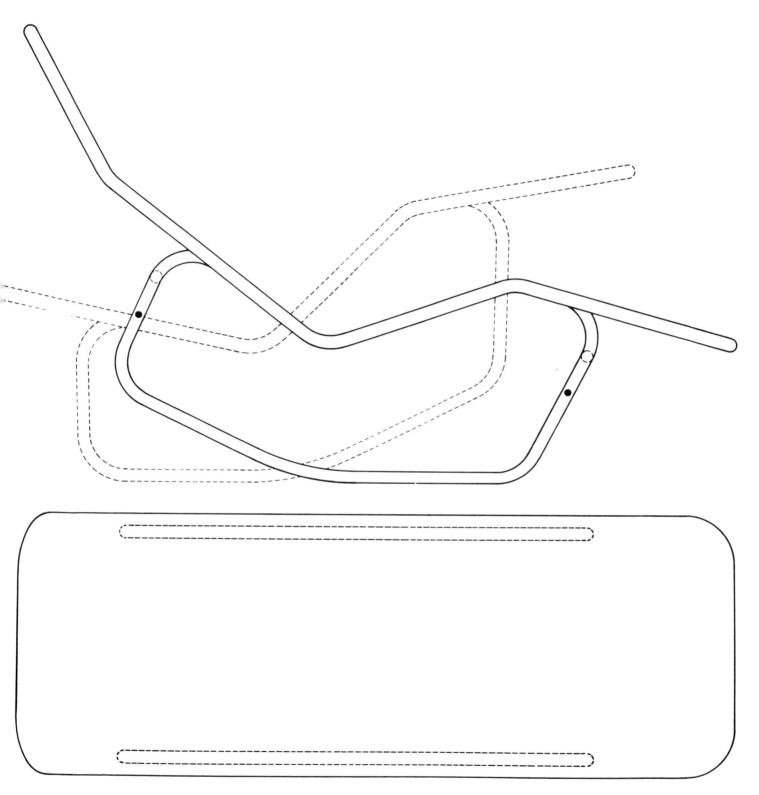

The DAR chair, with a variety of finishes and leg frames. This is Eames' classic dining or office chair, infinitely adaptable to its surroundings. The shell uncovered has a beautiful smooth contact surface, and is very comfortable. It is offered in a range of colours. Minimal upholstery over the inner surface of the shell is covered in fabric or leather, with a neatly finished line round the rim of the form. Chromium-plated legs are used, joined to the shell by Eames' rubber padded connectors, or columnar bases with or without castors.

Dining chairs
Charles Eames
U.S.A., 1949–63

I am treating this group of chairs as a chair-making system, rather than as individual classics, partly because Eames himself approaches the problem of chair designing in this way. He regards the seat element as a shell that should be contoured to the human body and the leg structure as a quite distinct base, to which the shell is attached. He has evolved a whole set of interchangeable shells and supports, producing a wide range of possible permutations. Starting out first with a fibreglass reinforced plastic shell, with or without armrests, he added an armless wire mesh (now no longer in production) which could be either partially or fully upholstered. Later he made low-backed versions of these for the Fonda del Sol restaurant in New York, and also, for airport seating, a series of bases with tubular beam and cast legs.

A more recent series of designs, under the name of the Aluminium Group, uses a number of cast aluminium frame elements holding a heat-sealed pad of fabric, foam and synthetic leather in resilient tension in narrow horizontal seamed bands. This group includes low and high-backed chairs and lounge chairs, all with or without arms and all adaptable to several different swivel bases.

The construction of the complete chair is particularly interesting in Eames' work, in that he has spent a great deal of effort experimenting to find satisfactory methods of joining his elements together. His most often used method of joining a seat to its base was revolutionary at its inception. It consists of a rubber casting chemically bonded to the shell with a nut embedded in it, to form the connection with the base. This allows a vital degree of flexibility between the two parts. It has been pointed out by Peter Smithson that, 'Before Eames no chairs (of the modern canon) were many-coloured or really light in weight, or not fundamentally rectangular in plan (i.e. the chairs of Rietveld,

Stam, Breuer, Le Corbusier, Mies, Aalto). Eames' chairs belong to the occupants not to the building. (Mies chairs are especially of the building and not of the occupants . . .) They use aluminium castings and wire struts which remind one (but only if one thinks about it) of new and old aeroplanes, not of other furniture. A lot of energy has been poured into their detail: it is workmanlike, explicit, even eloquent, but it is quiet'. This detail that Smithson mentions is designed to be highly appropriate to mass production techniques. All the welds Eames uses are electric resistance welds, and are not executed by hand. A resistance weld is an instantaneous process which requires no hand finishing, is elegant and structurally very sound when appropriately used. The variations possible with the seat shells, plus the range of upholstery materials, from self-coloured plastic to wool fabrics, can produce chairs to suit almost any combination of function, mood and colour scheme. Even where padded covers are used, they are always a separate and removable element. Also, the bases come either chromed or black, extending a further range of alternatives.

All these chairs have undergone continual modifications, additions and elaborations, to fit them for new functions: an example is the extra thick padding added to the back of the armless plastic shell when it is intended for use as a typing chair. Eames' aesthetic, both as an architect and as a designer of furniture, developed directly from a highly personal approach to functional considerations. It is unfortunate that these chairs, so carefully and successfully adapted to real mass-production, have still not achieved the recognition and the popularity that would enable them to be produced in the large numbers that would keep them at a moderate price. They are still made by the original manufacturer, Herman Miller, a very high quality company, using semi-mass production methods and selling through designers and architects to a limited luxury market.

In 1958, Eames produced his Aluminium Group: chairs with a single fine seat/back element, in horizontally seamed fabric or vinyl coverings over vinyl-coated fabric, over vinyl foam. This element, with its cast aluminium supporting frame, was used with a wide variety of bases, and at different angles and heights, producing an extremely flexible range of chairs, suited to every conceivable purpose.

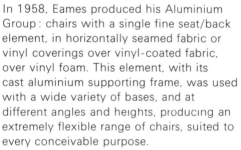

The DSS chair, with chromium-plated leg frame and with a splay-footed columnar base. This chair, with the DAR, was designed about 1950. It is made by Herman Miller International. The DSS was also made with linking leg frames, for multiple seating. With the chromium plated four-leg frame, it is a stacking chair.

THE chair

Hans Wegner

Denmark, 1949

This is perhaps the best known of Wegner's extensive range of chair designs. It epitomizes the characteristic qualities of his work — classicism, sophistication, a finely drawn structure and impeccably finished traditional materials. The design is simple, beautifully proportioned and modulated — it appears effortless, but is the result of a long and painstaking development through models and proto-types. The wide seat is a woven cane membrane: the chair is also available with an upholstered seat.

While all the parts seem to flow into each other making a unified form, the transition from one part to the next is always expressed. In the case of the arm to leg connection, for example, this is achieved by a slight recess at the joint which also prevents any unsightly shifting caused by the possible shrinkage of the wood. There is an elegant and ingenious finger joint connecting the arms to the backrest.

Wegner is not primarily concerned with the architectural aspects of chair design, nor with innovation for its own sake. His ideas flow more from the chair as it emerged from the nineteenth century. The design seems to have an affinity with the Arts and Crafts movement furniture and with the Riemerschmid chair (p. 25). His designs have been influential, in Scandinavia particularly, where there has been an apparently endless succession of refinements to a simple chair structure, mostly using fine woods, leather, canvas and cane.

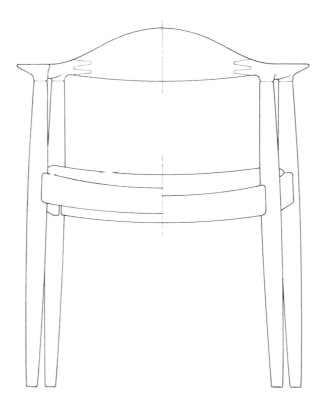

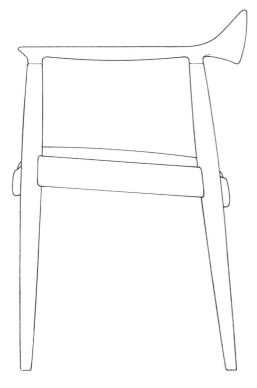

A version of Wegner's THE chair with a leather seat.

116

T chair

**William Katavolos,
Ross Litell,
Douglas Kelly**
U.S.A., 1953

One of the most significant team efforts in furniture design has been the range of pieces of which this is the key example. Each piece clearly expresses the philosophy of the design group, which was concerned with elegant proportioning, clarity of structure and an approach to the unity of form that was described as 'similarity in the differences and differences in the similarities'. Applied to this chair, this means that all the elements, whatever their function, are topologically the same, a T, and that all the T's are quite different from each other both in their orientation and their materials. Thus, we have three chromed-steel rod T's in two planes, a black bar T in a third, horizontal, plane, and a leather T plane lying in a curve. Every dimension falls in a constantly recurring proportion (the 'golden mean'), the final touch of elegance being the scroll-shaped connections between the leather and the frame, which are made by screwing the halved rods of the frame together from the top, and clamping the leather between them, before the legs are connected to the horizontal brace. Then, when the leather wraps over the top of the turned bars, it conceals all the screws. A subtle concession to comfort, which turns out to be also a subtle aesthetic refinement, is the slight curve in the back support bar. Besides adding greatly to the comfort of the chair, it introduces a shallow curve in opposite plane to the seat/back curve, again emphasizing the different alignments in which similar forms are structurally combined.

This chair shows interestingly the results of imposing preconceived decisions on the logic of forms in combination, in such a functional structure as a chair.

118

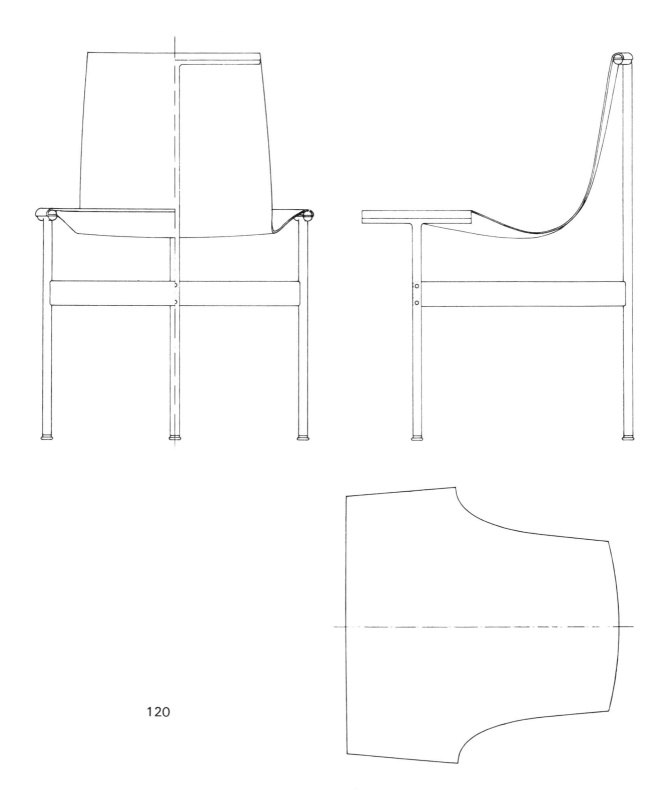

120

Lounge chair 670
Charles Eames
U.S.A., 1956

The only chair that Eames designed to achieve comfort both actual and psychological, this chair consists of a metal base which supports curved plywood parts made from rosewood, which in turn cradle the upholstered elements. These are made from soft leather covering down which is placed in turn over foam rubber. The design was made with the psychology of comfort very much in view. Thus the leather is permanently wrinkled by the way in which the buttons are placed, to suggest that it has recently been sat in; and the chair has generous proportions — its elements placed and angled in a way which indicates the comfort to come. There is a flexibility in the ingenious rubber connections between the headrest, backrest and seat via the armrest and the seat's base. The swivel and tilt mounted base of the chair has five prongs which enable it to sit in any position without looking off-centre. The chair is so comfortable that people who own it say that they find it virtually impossible to read complex texts while sitting in it.

It has had an incredible effect on the furniture industry, almost every manufacturer running to his designer for an equivalent chair in order to compete, almost all variations being reminiscent of the original.

It seems that so far no one has succeeded in designing an equivalent chair which gets away from the appearance of the Eames original. Nor has anyone succeeded in equalling its appearance of comfort. Aesthetically, this chair expresses comfort in the strongest possible way through visual means.

Perhaps the least aesthetically satisfying element of this chair is its base which like most bases used by Eames tends to look like a separate entity, bearing very little relation to the chair as a whole. It could obviously be used to support a table or any other piece of furniture or be interchangeable with a different chair. This was realized I think by Eliot Noyes when he designed his Xerox showroom and used Eames' chairs remounted on tubular bases which were simply inserted into the floor. This very much improved their appearance.

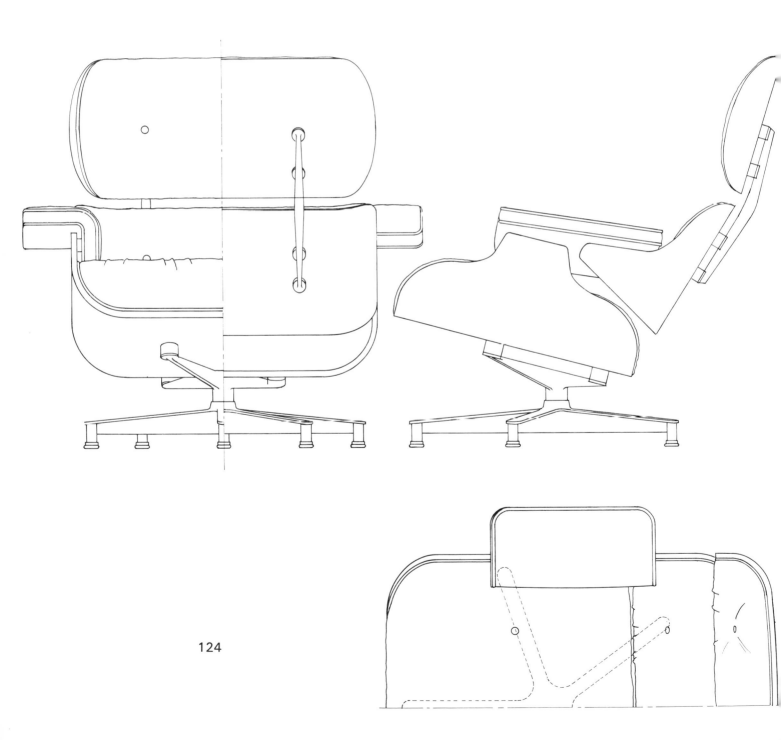

124

An experimental plywood chair,
designed by Eames about 1944. The
eventual separation of each plywood
element removed the need for the overlapping, but the contours of the 670 can
be discerned in this earlier model.

125

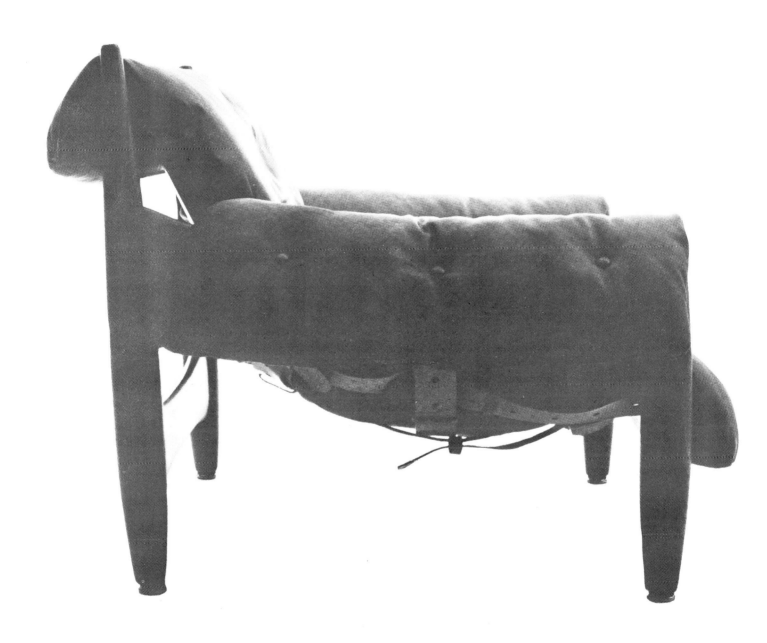

Sheriff chair
Sergio Rodriguez
Brazil, 1958

This chair has a rigid wooden frame, supporting a basket of loose interlaced hanging straps. These in turn support a single cushion element, seamed into seat, back and arm pads, which drapes over the frame allowing the body to hang, as it were, in an upholstered hammock-like basket. The low sturdy frame is made of polished teak; the leather straps are pegged into it, and can be adjusted to alter the tension of the membrane. Great freedom of movement is allowed for in this design. The Sheriff is perhaps derived from the notoriously uncomfortable family of sling chairs, but in this case the anatomical considerations have been superbly handled, and the result is a chair that not only looks extremely inviting and comfortable, but is so.

The Sheriff chair is one of the few modern chairs to have a completely informal appearance; it looks large and important but slouchingly casual, like a millionaire who wears faded Levis. Surprisingly rare in the modern idiom is the way this chair's appearance promises comfort, as does the creased leather of Eames' 670 chair. While many modern chairs are in fact made very comfortable, few of them give any visual value to this, because their support systems are cleverly concealed, and their contact surfaces are usually pristine.

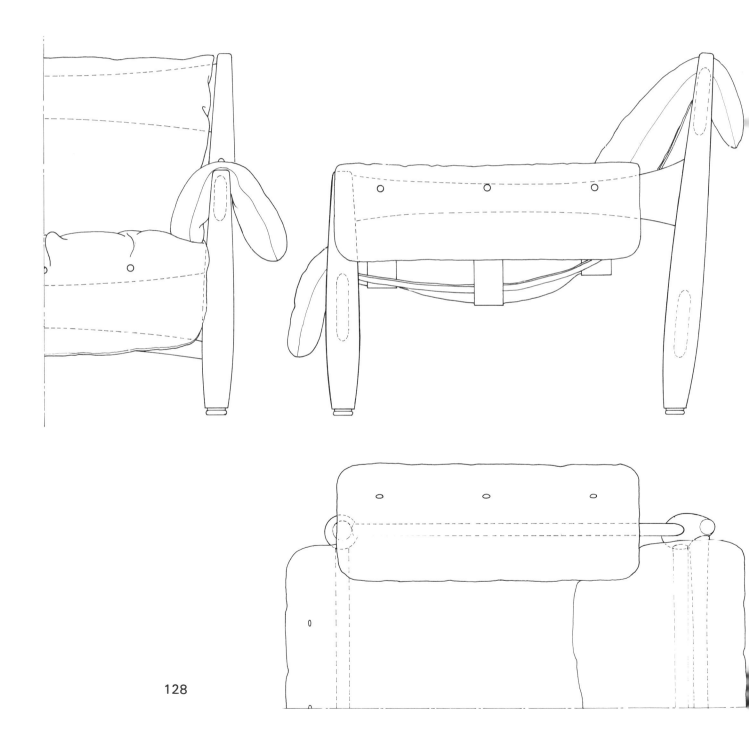

Panton stacking chair
Verner Panton
Switzerland, 1960

This is the first single form plastic chair, and is still one of the most satisfying and sensible. Whether or not there was any direct influence, Panton's chair bears a striking resemblance to Gerrit Rietveld's Zig-zag, designed in 1934, in its distribution of load and stress through one single cohesive form. Eero Saarinen's attempts to make a chair at least appearing to be all of one piece may have influenced Panton, but this design has itself certainly been very influential. Few designers, however, have achieved such a logical shape, in terms of comfort and strength of structure. Like all Panton's designs it has, in spite of great fluidity of line, a tightness of form rarely found in any plastic or glass-fibre structure. There is a trace of the formal vocabulary of the Art Nouveau style, in the slightly disconcerting way in which the chair seems to grow out of the floor. In this design, the freedom allowed by advances in plastics and mould-forming technology has been exploited to maximum advantage, but with a fine degree of restraint. The form is generous, but strictly functional.

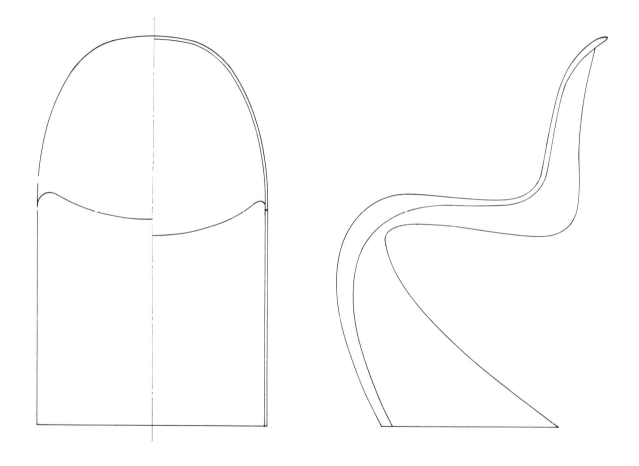

132

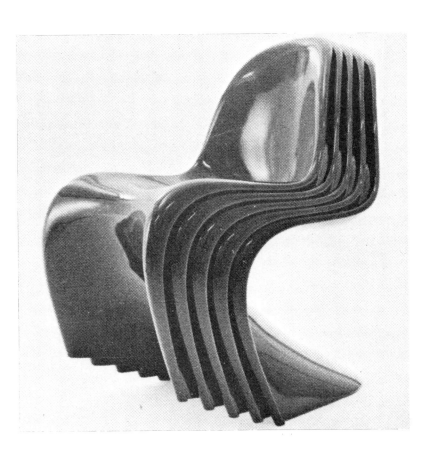

A group of Panton chairs, tightly
nested for storage.

Armchair 19
Vico Magistretti
Italy, 1960

Although ostensibly a 'folksy' traditional chair, on close examination this turns out to be one of the few truly modern designs in plain wood construction (as distinct from bentwood forms). The extreme strength of the chair is centred in the large leg cross-section at seat level, where the horizontal members interlock in a complex double mortice and tenon.

The shaping of the members is a completely straightforward expression of the structural idea. It is interesting to compare the Magistretti Armchair 19 with Hans Wegner's solution to the same problem. Both concentrate the strength of the chair in a thickening of the legs, both have woven seats and a single bar back rest. However, aesthetically they could not be less alike.

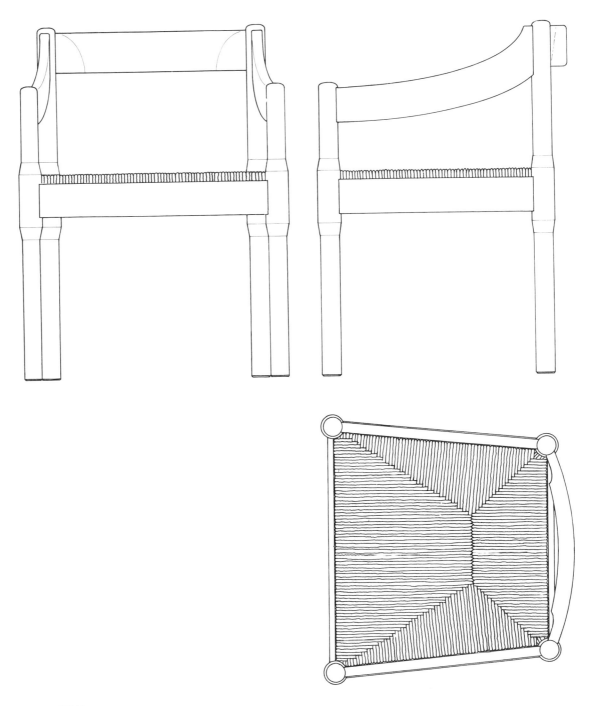

de chair and stool from the same series as the classic Magistretti armchair.

Armchair 12
Poul Kjaerholm
Denmark, 1962

This chair is made up of two bent steel tubes forming legs, arms and back, fixed to a flat-section steel seat frame. This is filled with a flat seat pad, upholstered in natural canvas, or either parchment or ox-hide, with a matching braided cover on the top back rung. The structure relies entirely on the strength of the seat frame, to hold the other two elements. This chair has been influenced by Thonet's bentwood forms, but it embodies a fresh use of the properties of tubular steel. There has been a revival of interest in the past few years in the use of tubular steel for furniture construction, and this is a good example, considering how many of the recent attempts have resulted in vulgarized versions of earlier classics. I find this a rather uncomfortable chair, as the back rung cuts painfully across the spine, but it is undoubtedly a beautiful chair. The apparently simple spatial arrangement of the elements, with curving lines around the wide flat seat, makes for a very finely proportioned structure.

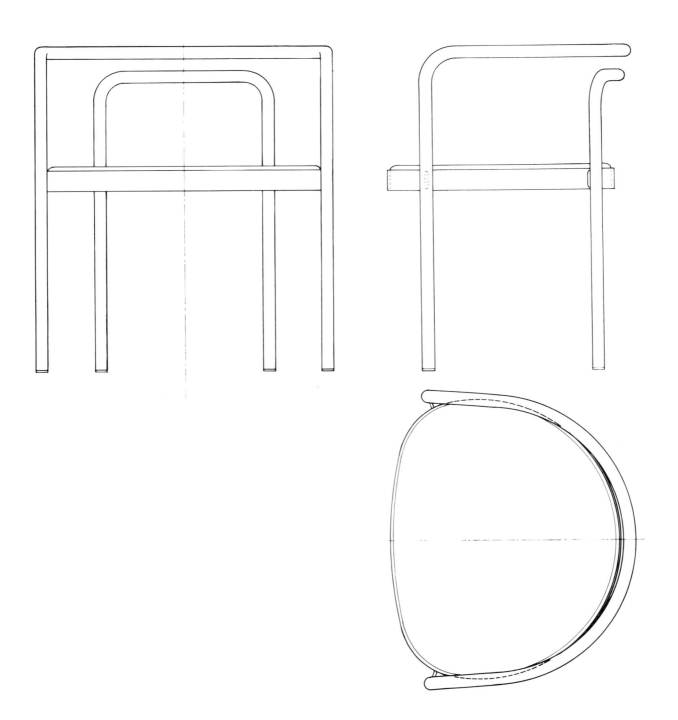

B-167-3 Lounge chair
Pierre Paulin
Holland, 1962

The shape of this chair is much more functional than a casual inspection would perhaps suggest. The basis of the structure is three tubular steel rings, for the rim, seat and base held by two verticals at the sides of the chair and laced with rubber strips. The inside surface and the rim are upholstered with foam rubber, but for the external area the stretched fabric cover creates its own contour by its tension over the frame. The moulded foam seat cushion sits in the small ring supported by the rubber webbing membrane. For a small, relatively unobtrusive chair, this is unusually comfortable. It is interesting to compare the surface curves, and the profile of this chair with the second of Gaetano Pesce's Up range. Paulin's chair is much more restrained, and has a rather more casual and inviting look.

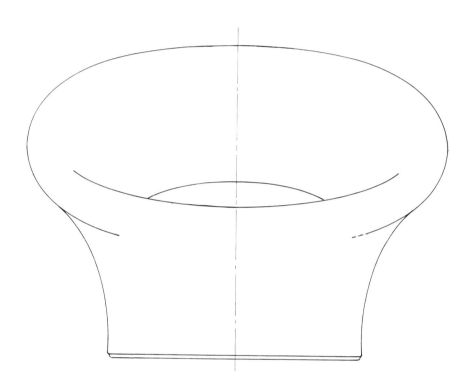

144

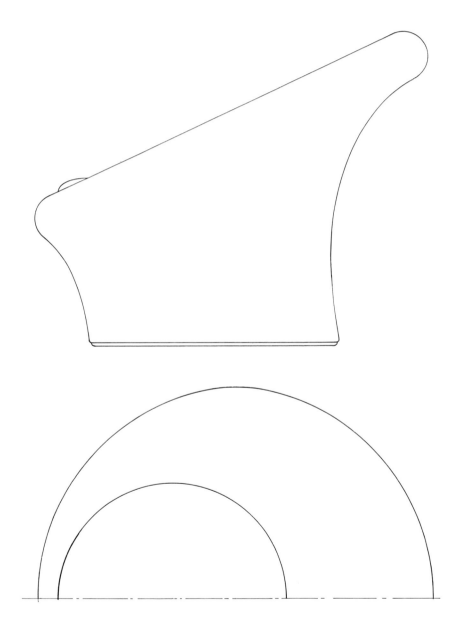

Sling chair
Clement Meadmore
U.S.A., 1963

The design of this chair grew out of an interest in the possibility of using the sling principle in an anatomically correct fashion, and in a way which would intrinsically include armrests. The steel structure consists of three parts: the back brace and uprights welded into a single unit, and the two front elements, each of which is attached with two screws, thus locking the leather sling in place.

The extended flat steel strips, seamed into the leather sling at each side, repeat the principle of the base, and it is this construction method that distinguishes this chair from others using a similar base, but supporting a conventionally upholstered seat and back. Because the leather is in a loose sling form, seamed between the seat and back contact areas, there is no stretching in use, and no restriction of body movement, even though the sling is virtually form fitting. It is as comfortable as many more complex padded and upholstered chairs. Both functionally and aesthetically the metal and leather elements are sufficiently closely integrated to form a unified whole.

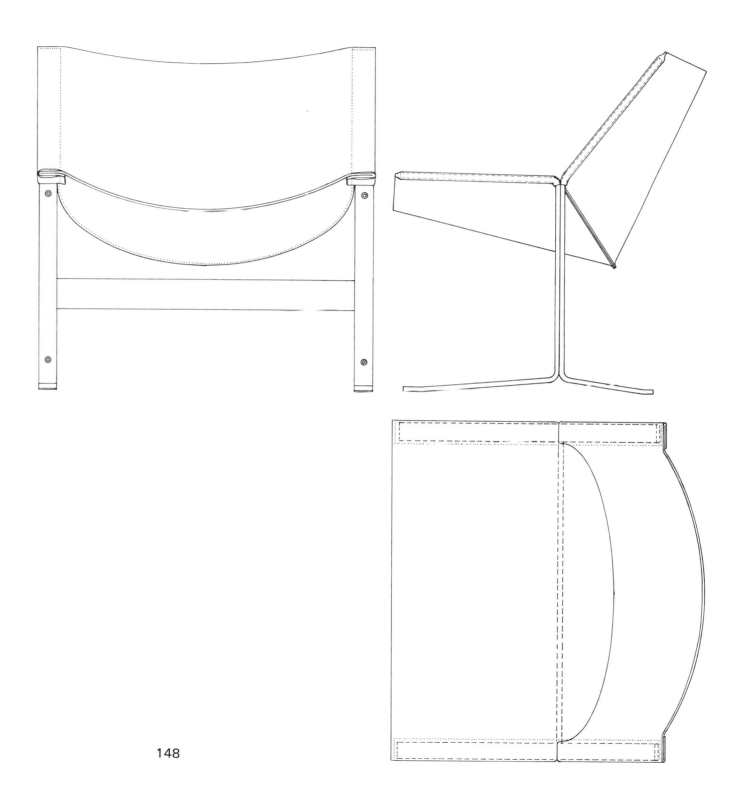

148

Sofa

George Nelson

U.S.A., 1963

I am including this, a sofa, in a book of chairs, because I consider it the only sofa to rank with the chairs selected for this book, as a classic design. As it happens, it is, to date, the only sofa chosen by the Museum of Modern Art in New York for its contemporary design collections. The sofa has chromium-plated steel tube legs, and cushions lying on rubber membranes within a round-cornered rectangular framing loop also in tubular steel. There are many aspects of Nelson's design that are especially ingenious. For example, the use of epoxy resin for the final assembly of the frame components. This enables welded elements like the connector between the front and back legs, or the T-shaped sections connecting the main loop with its ends, to be mass-produced. The epoxy connection is used to put together elements making up sofas of various lengths, as required. The method of supporting the cushions, consisting of a series of neoprene rubber platforms stretched between the front and back cross bars, is very simple and highly effective. The cushions themselves are leather-covered dacron and foam with a single welt around the edges. The leather is pre-formed into a curve at the corners, which gives a soft, rounded shape.

The effect of all this careful detailing, combined with a strong original design idea, is a sofa that for once does not look like an extended version of a chair, nor a vast and unwieldy piece of upholstery. It is a very taut design, embodying the best of new design principles, but still looking invitingly comfortable, mainly because of the soft shape of the cushions.

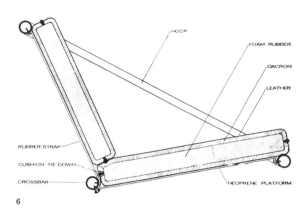

HOOP

FOAM RUBBER

DACRON

LEATHER

RUBBER STRAP

CUSHION TIE DOWN

CROSSBAR

NEOPRENE PLATFORM

6

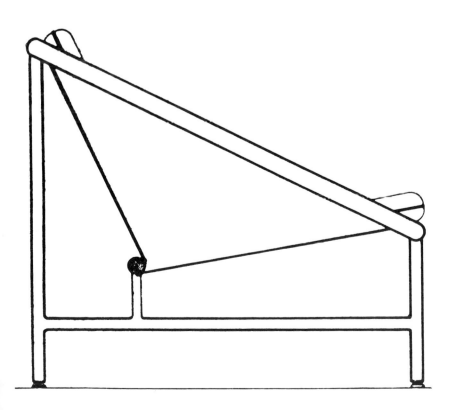

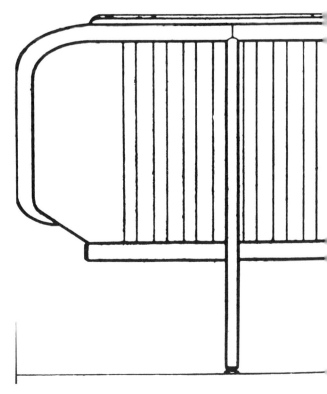

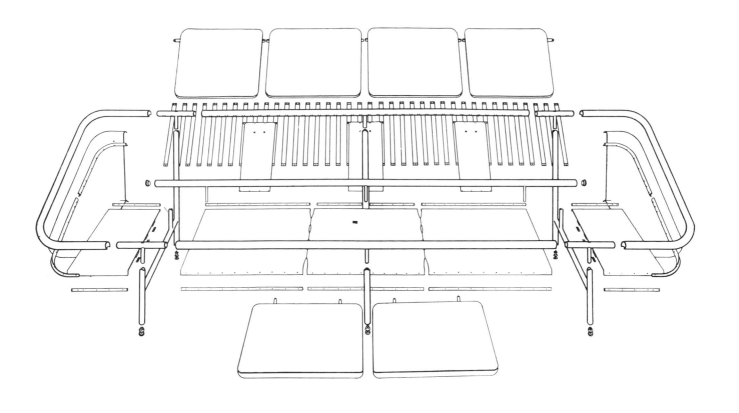

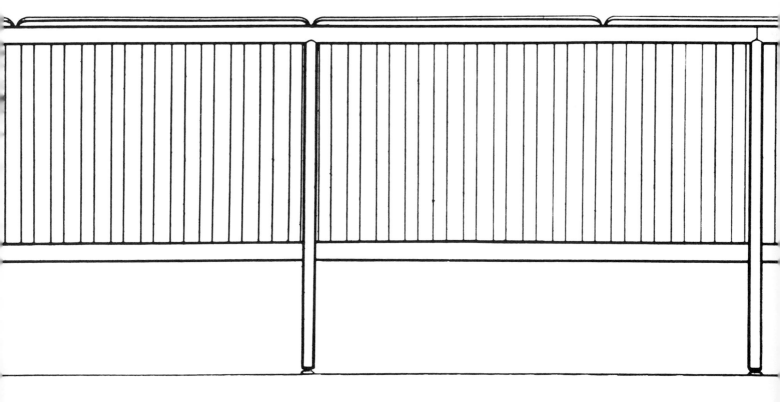

Steltman
Gerrit Rietveld
Holland, 1964

A recently discovered Rietveld design of unknown date, this is quite a different concept from his Red-Blue and Berlin chairs with their delineation of lines and planes in space. Here a series of 2″ × 4″ elements are butted together to form a series of L shapes which are then assembled in the familiar by-passing relationship used in the other chairs. Like the Zig-zag chair it has the appearance of being smaller than it is despite its bulky construction.

The Steltman, named after the client for which it was designed, is made in natural oak and is available in both left and right-handed versions.

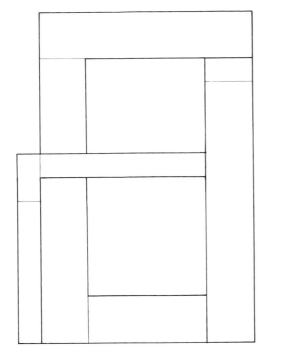

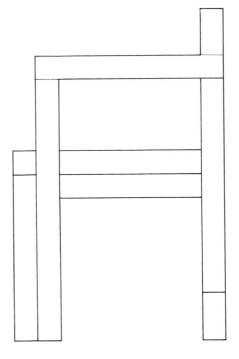

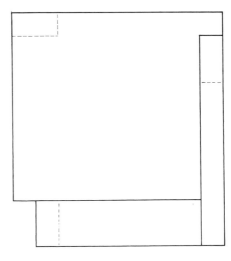

156

GF 40/4 stacking chair
David Rowland
U.S.A., 1964

The final design date for this chair is 1964, but the research and development of the chair itself, including special techniques and materials, began in 1956. David Rowland set out to tackle the basic criterion for a successful stacking chair, namely closeness of nesting. By using a very thin high-tensile steel rod with a sheet metal seat and back, he achieved a stacking distance of half an inch. This design is an outstandingly good solution to the problem of quantity stacking and storage, and has emerged as both a beautiful and a comfortable chair.

Lecture or conference hall seating is notorious, and the sight of this chair in an auditorium can be a great relief, as it has an unusually high standard of comfort, combined with a small but vital amount of flexibility under a fidgeting body.

The frame is made of a steel rod $\frac{7}{16}$" in diameter. The detailing is clean and direct. For example, all the joints are silver-brazed, a technique that gives a smooth perfectly formed weld requiring little or no finishing work before chrome-plating. The seat and back are made of formed sheet steel with $\frac{3}{16}$" rolled edges, adding with great economy of means to the chair's structural strength. Also, being set between the frames, rather than on them, the seat and back add no extra thickness of their own in terms of stacking distance. The specially developed vinyl coating on the sheet steel adds considerably to the chair's virtues, making a maintenance-free finish, giving a pleasant non-metallic feel to the contact areas, and allowing a range of colours to be offered. Also, the chair is completely fireproof.

A special trolley is available with the GF 40/4, with strong castor wheels, allowing for the easy movement of a stack of forty of the chairs at a time. It is

A stack of thirty David
Rowland stackers, on their custom-
made trolley.

worth noting that such a stack is only four feet high overall. Flanges on the back of the frame incorporate male and female connectors for interlocking lines of chairs. The front connection is made through floor glides that are almost invisible, being made of clear plastic. The interlocking system is firm enough to allow for four chairs at a time to be gang-stacked for fast clearance. The flanges on the legs are the only slightly disturbing element of the chair, but they are necessary for structural stiffening, and have been handled with subtlety. To say that this chair has influenced subsequent designs would be a gross understatement. Manufacturers, aware of the demand for large-capacity movable seating, and for economically stored flexible seating for all purposes, are driving their designers to produce a competitor with these stringent specifications. No other design has yet achieved the beautiful simplicity and total appropriateness of Rowland's chair.

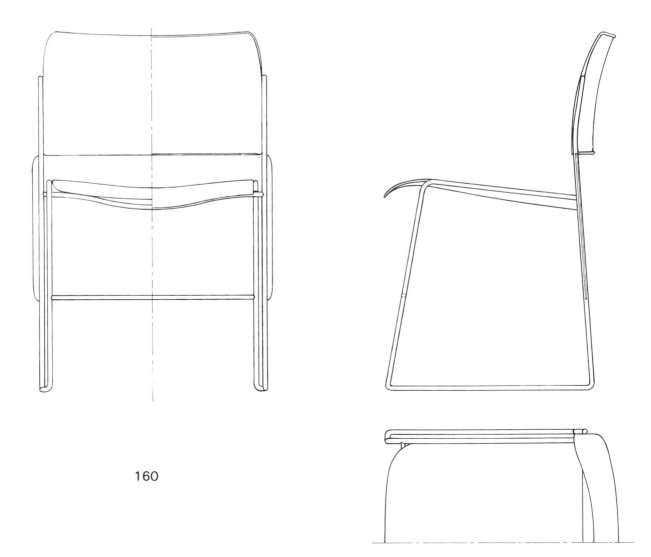

160

162

Chair 932
Mario Bellini
Italy, 1967

Bellini's aim in designing Chair 932 was to create an interchangeable system whereby cushions could be arranged to form a one, two or three seat chair, simply by adding further cushions and putting a longer belt around them. Le Corbusier's Grand Confort, with its use of large unconnected cushions simply held in position, influenced this design, but his rigid frame did not allow for rearrangement or extension. There is a similar satisfaction, however, in seeing the undisguised construction of the chair.

The new and unique aspect of this design is the connecting belt. It passes through wide flat loops stitched into the leather covering of each cushion, and so their position, and therefore their function within the chair, is not interchangeable.

This opulent chair, without any conventional structure, could be built in a traditional upholstery workshop. Bellini's design has come at a time when such luxurious shapes are in use again. Perhaps we have overcome the widespread mid-century reaction against the heavily upholstered furniture of the inter-war period, and can now again accept luxury seating of this sort.

Other chairs and sofas of the range
designed by Mario Bellini, with more
cushions linked by the same strap.

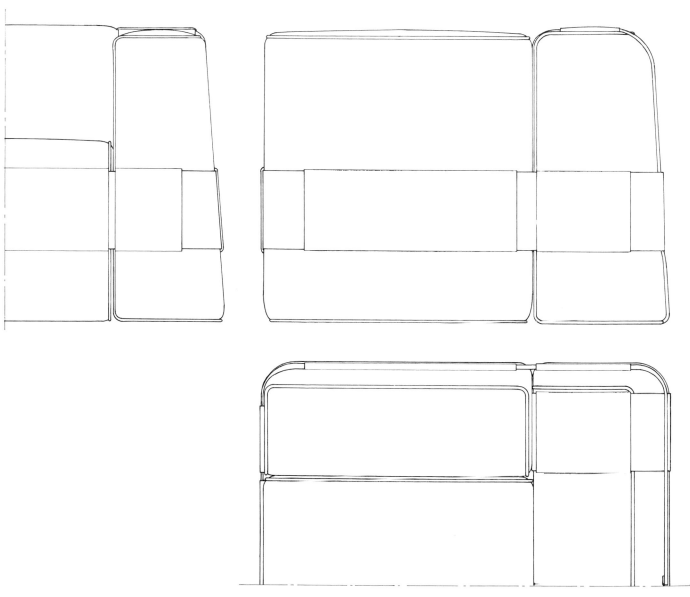

Chair 20

Poul Kjaerholm
Denmark, 1968

This chair is obviously developed from the Triennale chair: the supporting elements have all been simplified and the tension system is more explicit. The side frames of the seat and back, and the leg units (cantilevers) are all connected to a single transverse steel yoke, which is slightly bent, this springs the side frames outward, and these are then brought back into alignment by the tension of the leather covering. Thus the covering is kept permanently taut by the spring of the yoke. In the case of the Triennale chair this spring system only applies to the backrest, whereas here, with Chair 20, the whole seat and back as a unit is under a permanent tension. Visually the chair shares the same elegant gracefulness as all Kjaerholm's recent designs, and as usual shows an ingenious use of materials, and an ability to simplify the elements while retaining various functional advantages in the way these elements are used.

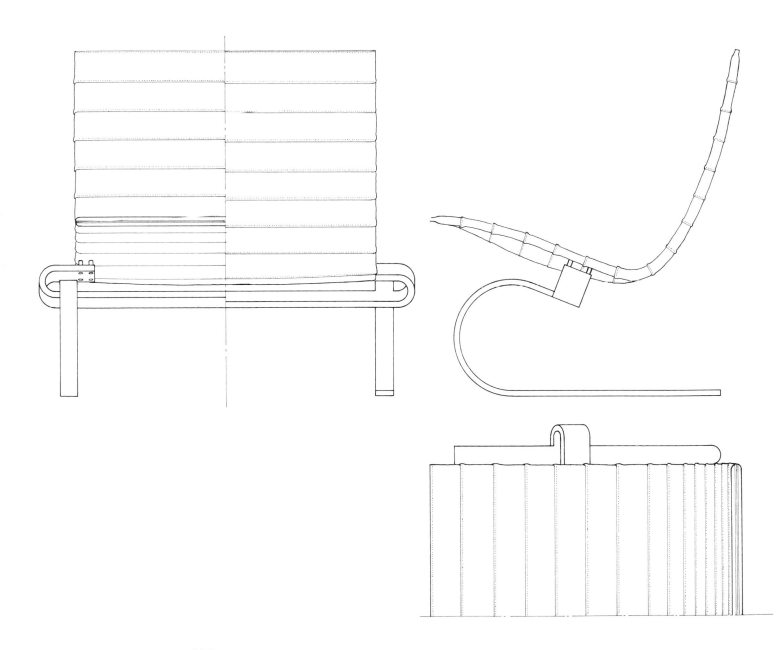

168

Pastilli
(also called Gyro)
Eero Aarnio
Finland, 1968

This chair is a two-part glass fibre casting, seamed around the perimeter of the form. It is made in a selection of bright colours, and is clearly intended to be enjoyed as much as possible by its owner and his children, rather than left in dignified isolation in an uninhabited sitting room. If one avoids rough rocks it can be used on the dunes and the beach, in the sea, and on snow. It is surprisingly comfortable for ordinary sitting purposes, and it rocks and gyrates freely on its rounded, unprotected bottom.

Aarnio has designed other similarly organic forms, notably the famous Globe chair, in which glass fibre seems to be pushed to its most generous extreme. There are no sharp concavities or sudden convolutions of form, in the Pastilli or the Globe, to interrupt the beautiful full-blown surface of the material.

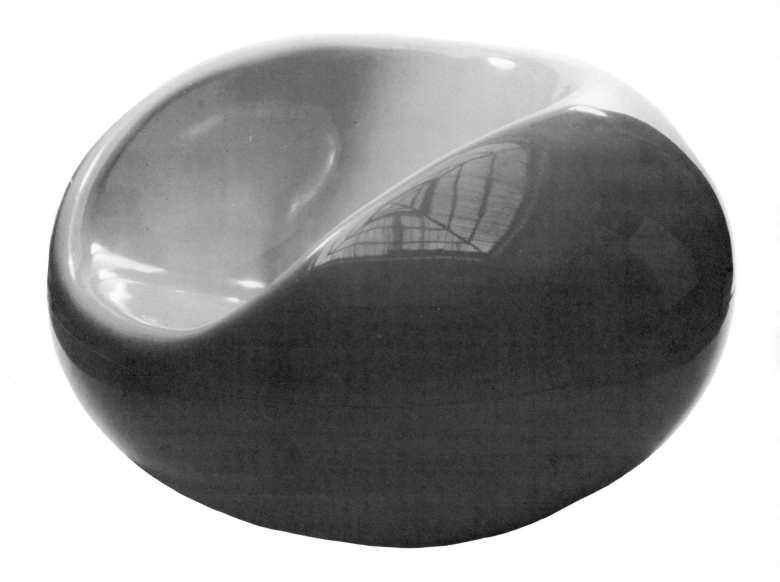

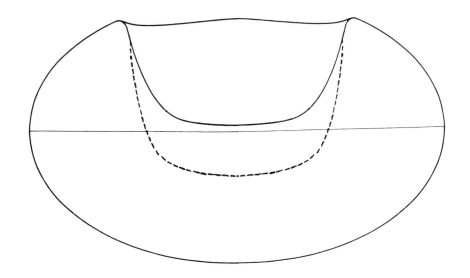

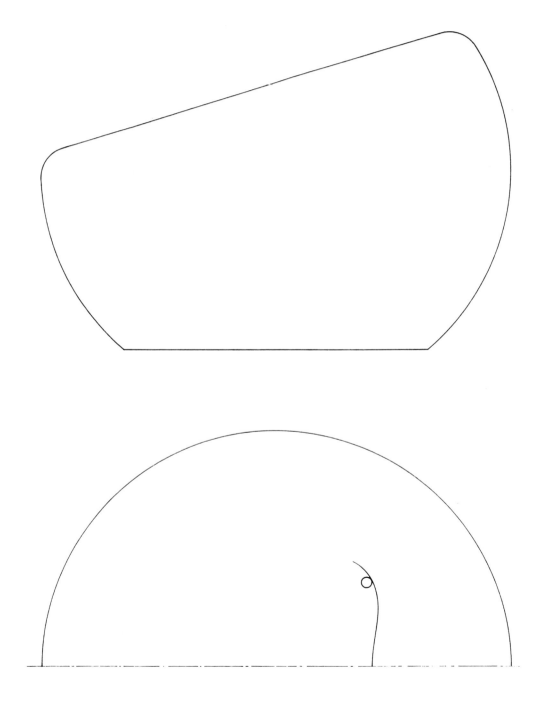

Up 1 chair

Gaetano Pesce

Italy, 1969

Gaetano Pesce is an architect, graphic artist and furniture designer. His Up 1 chair solved several problems in a unique and amusing way. The chair consists of polyurethane foam of a precisely controlled density, with a stretch nylon and wool jersey cover. The tailored cover is held into shape simply by the use of two buttons which are tied to a plywood base and which pull the back of the seat surface down into the foam. For shipping, the chair is placed in a vacuum chamber between sheets of vinyl. The air is withdrawn, the chair is compressed to a tenth of its original volume, the vinyl is then heat sealed, and packed in a flat box. When it is unsealed the foam expands back to its original size and shape by itself. This is one of the few organically shaped chairs which doesn't have the sort of modernistic shape reminiscent of Arp's sculpture of the Twenties. In this case the shape is a direct result of its function and construction therefore more satisfying than most of the fancy modellings we now see in plastics and foam.

It is one of the few important chairs which can be used casually in a room, without the feeling that it should be lined up with the adjacent walls and furniture.

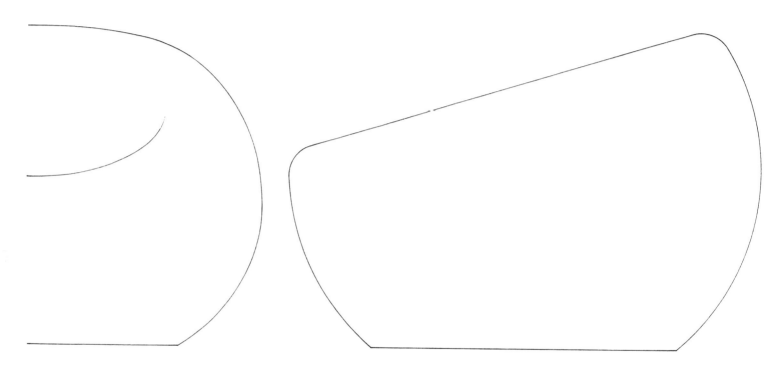

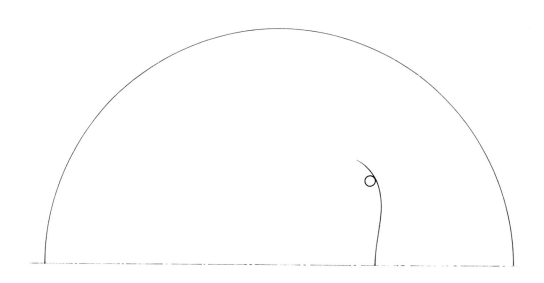

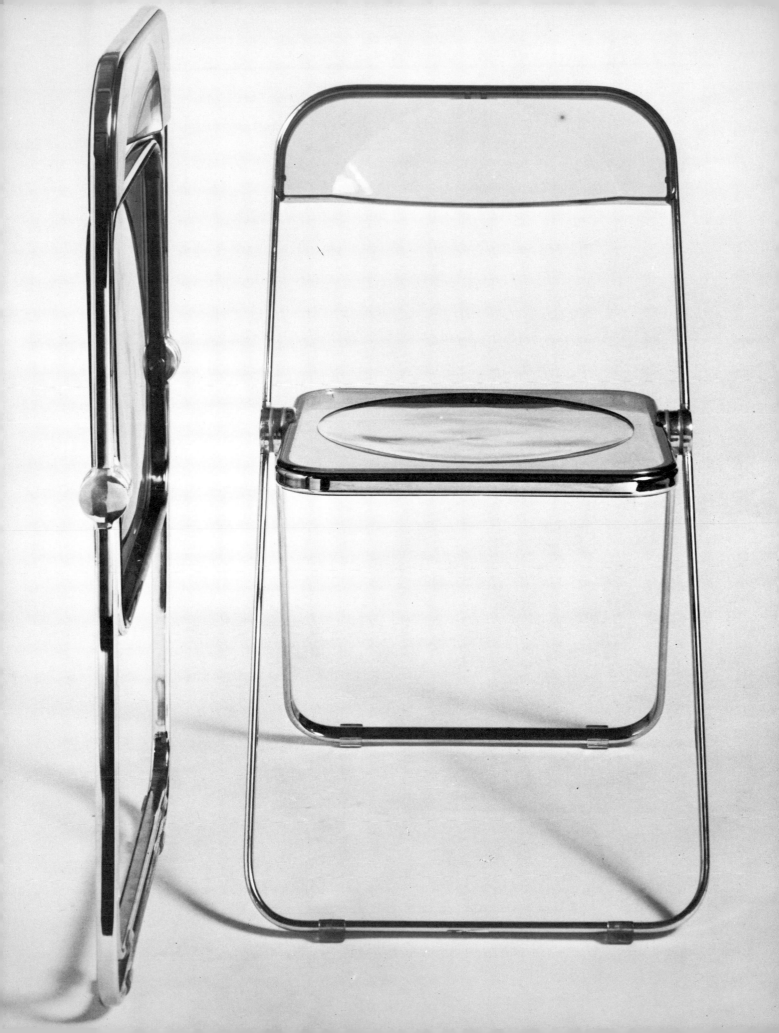

Plia

Giam Carlo Piretti
Italy, 1969

What used to be a humble folding wooden chair, has been transformed into a highly complex technological *tour de force* of gem-like visual simplicity. All the previously scattered mechanics have been concentrated in a single cast aluminium hub which also appears in an armchair and a desk by the same designer.

When folded, the chair is one inch thick except for the hub. The cast plastic seat and back elements come in opaque or translucent colours, white and plain. The frame is formed from an oval section tube which is chromed or plasticized in white.

This is not the original folding chair but it may be the final refinement of the whole idea.

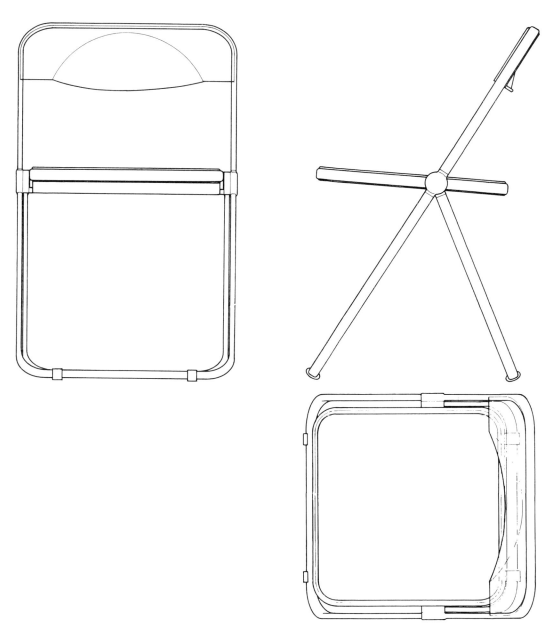

180

Soriana chair
Afra and Tobia Scarpa
Italy, 1970

The Scarpa's have here produced something close to the ultimate alternative to traditional upholstery. Upholstered chairs used to be made by skilled craftsmen, working with layers of padding on a timber frame. The chair has a minimal wooden base, supporting the polyurethane foam of which the chair is made. This foam is topped with a layer of soft dacron fibrefill, and a loose-fitting fabric or leather cover, shaped with a minimum of tailoring. The chair is given its final form by two chromium-plated steel wire clips. This simple but revolutionary system has been used to create a whole series of pieces, including an elongated chair, ottoman sofas and armchairs. Perhaps one has to have a certain taste for plumpness to like this chair, but it is hard to deny that it has a sensuous softness and disarming honesty of construction.

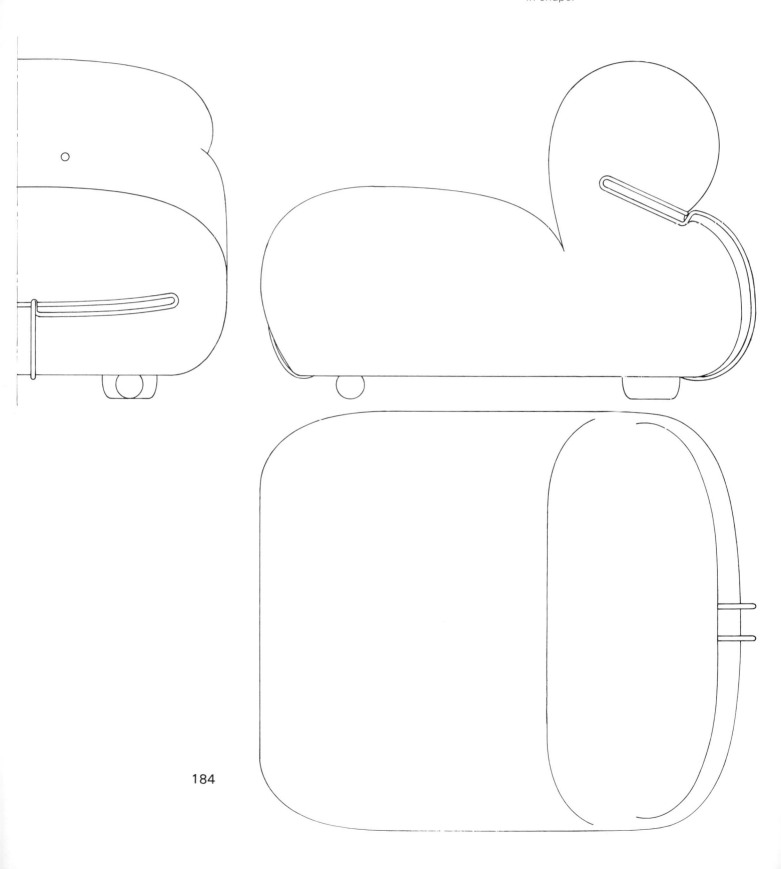

Front and back views of the Soriana
chair, showing the way in which the steel
wire clip holds the substance of the chair
in shape.

184

Appoggio
Claudio Salocchi
Italy, 1971

Designed for standing with some of the weight off one's legs in spaces too restricted for sitting, the Appoggio is anatomically shaped to correspond to the base of the pelvis. Probably taking his cue from the bicycle seat, Salocchi applied a knowledge of anatomy to the stool and came up with a design to solve space problems in kitchens, news theatres, public transport and so on. On some of these applications a fixed pole base plugged into the floor can be substituted for the free standing adjustable height arrangements shown.

One interesting feature is the method of height adjustment which consists of a screw which tightens into a groove in the sliding rod. In order to prevent the seat from dropping if the screw should loosen, the groove is cut deeper towards the bottom so that the application of weight causes a wedging effect against the screw. The height adjustment feature is important because unlike a chair the success of the Appoggio depends on its ability to match the length of a person's legs, the dimension of the human body which varies most from person to person.

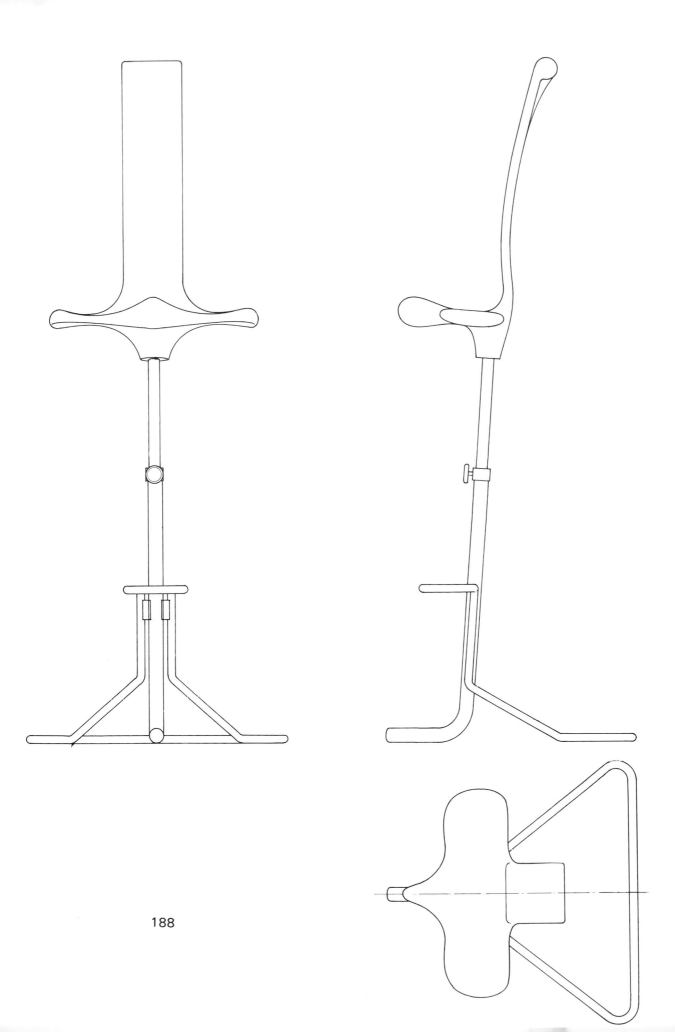

Biographies

Alvar Aalto
born 1898, Kuortane, Finland
architect, urban designer
trained Helsinki
own architectural office from
1923
taught Massachusetts Institute
of Technology
1940–49

Eero Aarnio
born 1923, Finland
interior and industrial designer
trained Helsinki
own office from 1962, Finland

Mario Bellini
born 1935, Italy
architect
trained Milan
own office from 1962, Milan

Marcel Breuer
born 1902, Hungary
architect, furniture designer
trained Bauhaus 1920–24
taught Bauhaus, 1924–28
own architectural office
1928–35
moved to England and
subsequently U.S.A.
from 1935
taught Harvard 1937–46
own office, New York, Paris
1956–

Charles Eames
born 1907, U.S.A.
architect, furniture and
industrial designer
trained Washington
own office from 1930
taught Cranbrook Academy
from 1936

William Katavolos, Douglas Kelly, Ross Littell
all born about 1929
industrial designers
worked as a team for Laverne,
New York 1948–50

Poul Kjaerholm
born 1929, Denmark
architect, furniture designer
trained Copenhagen
taught Copenhagen 1952–56
associated with E. Kold
Christensen

Le Corbusier
born 1887, died 1965
architect, artist, town planner,
writer
trained Switzerland
own architectural office from
1917
(see *My Work* published
1960)

Ross Littell
see William Katavolos

George Nelson
born 1907, New York
trained Yale University
own office from 1947
associated with Herman Miller
1947-65

Verner Panton
born 1926, Denmark
architect, designer
trained Copenhagen
collaborated with Arne
Jacobsen 1950-52
own office from 1955

Pierre Paulin
born 1927, Paris
designer
trained Paris
associated with Mobilier
National, Paris and Artifort,
Maastricht, Holland

Gaetano Pesce
born 1939, Italy
architect, graphic designer
trained Venice University
own office
associated with Group N,
Padua

Gerrit Rietveld
born 1888, died 1964, Holland
architect, furniture designer,
cabinet maker
trained Utrecht
own architectural office from
1919
member of De Stijl 1919-31
founder member of Congres
Internationaux d'Architecture
Moderne

Sergio Rodrigues
born 1927, Brazil
architect, furniture designer
own architectural office in Rio de
Janeiro

Mies van der Rohe
born 1886, Aachen, died 1969,
Chicago
architect
own architectural office from
1912
associated with the Deutsche
Werkbund 1926-32
Director of the Bauhaus
1930-33
moved to America 1938

David Rowland
born Los Angeles
industrial designer
trained Cranbrook Academy
of Art
own office from 1954

Tobia Scarpa
born 1935, Italy
architect, industrial designer
trained Venice University
glass designer 1958-60
own office with his wife Afra
from 1960

Vladimir Tatlin
born 1885, died 1953, U.S.S.R.
painter, designer, sculptor
founder of constructivism,
maker of flying devices,
revolutionary

Michael Thonet
born 1796, died 1871
inventor of the bentwood
process
founder of the firm Gebrüder
Thonet, Vienna

Hans Wegner
born 1914, Denmark
architect, designer
trained Copenhagen
own office from 1943

Manufacturers

Bentwood armchair
Gebrüder Thonet, Vienna

Tripolina
Citterio, Como, Italy

Riemerschmid chair
Dunbar Furniture Corporation,
Indiana

Folding chair
Simon International, Bologna,
Italy

Red-Blue chair
originally produced by G.A. van der
Groenekan, Holland, now also
Cassina, Milan

Berlin chair
G. A. van der Groenekan, Holland

Wassily chair
Gavina, Milan; distributed by
Knoll International

MR chair
originally produced by J. Muller,
Berlin; now by Gebrüder Thonet,
Knoll International and other
manufacturers

Tatlin chair
new production model by Nikol,
Italy

Cesca
Mannesmann Steel with the
Bauhaus; from 1965 Gavina,
Milan; distributed by Knoll
International

Basculant
originally made by Gebrüder
Thonet; now by Cassina, Milan;
distributed by Atelier International, N.Y.

Chaise longue
originally made by Gebrüder
Thonet; now by Cassina, Milan;
distributed by Atelier International, N.Y.

Barcelona chair
Knoll International

Tugendhat chair
manufactured and distributed by
Knoll International

Brno chair
Knoll International

Armchair 406
Artek, Helsinki
distributed by I.C.F.,N.Y.,U.S.A.

Zig-zag chair
G. A. van der Groenekan, Holland;
now Cassina, Milan; distributed
by Atelier International, N.Y.

Easy chair
Cado, Denmark

Landi
P & W Blattman, Zurich

LCM chair
Herman Miller International
Collection

Barwa chaise
Finkel Outdoor Products, Inc.,
U.S.A.

Dining chairs
Herman Miller International
Collection

THE chair
Johannes Hansen, Copenhagen;
distributed by Design Selections
International, N.Y.,U.S.A.

T Chair
Laverne International, New York;
Wilhelm Bofinger, Stuttgart

Lounge chair 670
Herman Miller International
Collection

Sheriff chair
OCA, Rio de Janeiro

Panton stacking chair
Herman Miller International
Collection

Armchair 19
Cassina, Milan; Distributed by
Design Selections International,
N.Y.

Armchair 12
E. Kold Christensen A/S,
Copenhagen; distributed by
Design Selections International,
N.Y.,U.S.A.

B-167-3 Lounge chair
Artifort, Maastrict

Sling chair
distributed by Design Selections
International, N.Y.,U.S.A.

Sofa
Herman Miller International
Collection

GF 40/4 stacking chair
General Fireproofing, U.S.A.

Chair 932
Cassina, Milan; distributed by
Atelier International, N.Y.

Chair 20
E. Kold Christensen A/S,
Copenhagen; distributed by
Design Selections International,
N.Y.

Pastilli
also called Gyro; Asko, Lahti,
Finland; distributed by Stendig,
N.Y.

Up 1 chair
B & B Italia, Como, Italy

Plia
Castelli, Bologna and New York

Soriana chair
Cassina, Milan; distributed by
Atelier International, N.Y.

Appoggio
Sormani, Como, Italy; distributed
by Castelli, N.Y.

Index